D1824231

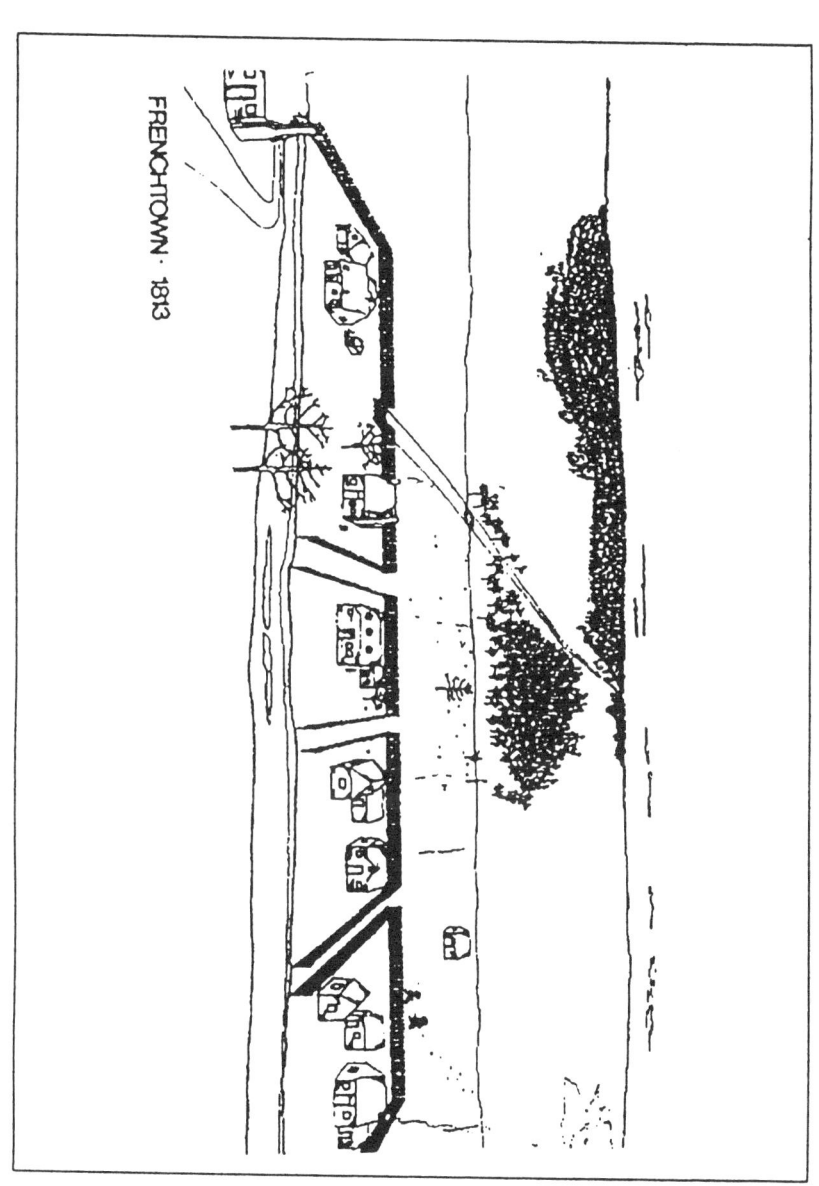

FRENCHTOWN · 1813

Escape to Frenchtown

A Narrative of the War of 1812
at the River Raisin

by
Ralph Naveaux
and
Rachel Wilkie

Ralph Naveaux

iii

This Edition Published by

The Monroe County Historical Society

P. O. Box 665
Monroe, MI 48161

First Printing   -   1000 copies

Copyright 2000:   **Monroe County Historical Commission**

ISBN 0-615-11452-0

This book is dedicated to
the Memory of

Edwin L. Long
1902-1991

whose research and artistic efforts
contributed to
our 20th century study and interpretation
of the historic events which occurred
at the River Raisin

Acknowledgements

The authors would like to thank Dr. John Laboe and Lynn Reaume for their help, advice, and encouragement in writing this book.

Dr. Laboe is a descendent of René LeBeau. He kindly shared his research in genealogy and family history with us. Mrs. Reaume, Archival Assistant at the Monroe County Historical Museum, provided her insights into the early community and the early Catholic Church in Monroe.

Most of the artwork was contributed by Lynn Reaume and Joe Lee, a long-time friend and supporter of historical projects. We appreciate their permission to use their drawings in illustrating this book. Any copyright for other uses of their work is retained by the artists, themselves.

Our thanks also goes to Museum Director Matt Switlik and Educational Coordinator Sue Rodich for their support and technical suggestions.

In addition to general reference books, the authors made extensive use of primary sources found in the Monroe County Historical Museum Archives.

Outside the cost of production, all proceeds from this work go to support historical programs in Monroe County.

Table of Contents

Fact or Fiction?

This story has been fictionalized. However, it is based on historic fact. The people in the story are real. They actually existed. Their names and identities have not been changed. They lived during a very exciting (and also very dangerous) time in the history of our community. Moreover, for this brief moment, our local history took center stage in the drama of our nation.

Unfortunately, not everything that was done or said by our early settlers was documented. We, the authors, had to use our imaginations to fill in the gaps. By dramatizing the story, we also hoped to interest those for whom history is normally just a dry recitation of the facts.

Our most mysterious and most fictionalized character is Etienne LeBeau. We do not know if he was present at all the places we put him, but we used him as a tool so that you could see the Battle of the River Raisin through his eyes.

By way of contrast, we had much more information on Etienne's brother, Alexis, and his sister, Genevieve. If anything, there were too many accounts of their tragic flight on the night of January 18, 1813. We had to sort through a mass of conflicting details to come up with the most likely historical version. Other details of their adventure are sketchy, however. We don't really know where they stayed after the 18th, or how they got to Detroit.

Other characters appear as they are mentioned in historical records, personal memoirs, family stories, and later interviews. The Battle of the River Raisin was the most terrible and dramatic event our community has ever endured. We hope our story will give the reader some insight into what it was like to live here during those trying days of the War of 1812.

A Native Hunter, Summer, 1812
by Joe Lee

Introduction

Native-Americans inhabited the River Raisin area in prehistoric times. Early records tell of the mysterious *gens du feu,* or people of the fire. By the time the first French explorers reached the area, however, this tribe had disappeared. Perhaps they were related to the Potawatomi, who moved into southeastern Michigan after Cadillac established Detroit in 1701.

In mid century, the Potawatomies moved south, to a stream they called Namesibi,[1] or River of Sturgeon, their name for the River Raisin. They, in turn, began to attract a few Frenchmen. Although there are few records of intermarriage between the local French and Indians, many visitors to the area in later years remarked on the extent to which the French had "gone native."

French control came to an end when British troops arrived in 1760. Most of the French settlers chose to remain in the area as British subjects, even remaining neutral during the native uprising led by Chief Pontiac.

By the 1783 Treaty of Paris, Michigan and the "Old North West Territory" became part of the newly created United States of America. The attempts of the American Government to exercise control over the territory, however, were blocked by Native American resistance and by the presence of British troops at key points along the major fur trading routes.

About this same time, French-Canadians began migrating south from Detroit in large numbers, establishing narrow, ribbon shaped farms along the waterways draining into Lake Erie from the interior of Michigan. They found the River Raisin much the same as Fathers Hennepin and Charlevoix had described it during their journeys in the early decades of the 18th century. Its clear waters were teeming with fish and so crowded with waterfowl that the ducks would line up in order let the canoes pass. The riverbanks were overgrown with wild grapevines, which climbed high into the neighboring trees and gave the river its name in French, la Rivière aux Raisins.[2]

In 1784, 20-year-old Francois[3] Navarre became the first permanent white settler on the River Raisin. For many years he had traveled around the region, trapping and trading with the Indians, British, and Americans. He had, on many occasions, passed through the River Raisin area, sometimes by canoe, but often on horseback, using additional packhorses to carry his wares and furs.

On one particular trip, he encountered a Potawatomi chief who spent a rather long time admiring Navarre's horse. The chief told Navarre that he had dreamed that Navarre had given the horse to him as a gift. He added the fact that whatever an Indian dreamed must come true.

Navarre was familiar with native traditions and, in the interest of maintaining his profitable trading relationship, gave the chief his prized horse. However, on his next visit, he sought out the same chief and told him he had also had a dream that the Potawatomi had given him the land south of the river, all the way to Plum Creek.

The old Indian was pleased with Navarre's cunning and granted the land to him and his brother, Jacques, with the agreement that Navarre would have no more dreams. The land measured well over a thousand acres. The Potawatomies also gave Navarre a name, Tchigoy[4], and accepted him as a friend.[5]

Many others followed Navarre's lead. In defiance of British law, the French made personal deals with the Potawatomi, who were living in small villages, scattered across the River Raisin Country from the Huron River all the way to the Maumee in Ohio.

The new community prospered, with red man and white man living in relative harmony. Several miles up the River Raisin from Francois Navarre's house, the settlers, called *habitants,* built a Catholic Church named St. Antoine's or St. Anthony's.[6] It proved difficult, however, to find a priest who was willing and able to live in an isolated pioneer community. Much of the time the *habitants* had to rely on occasional visits by the priest from St. Anne's Church in Detroit.

The farms of the *habitants* stretched like ribbons, away from the banks of the Raisin and other streams, giving each family a narrow frontage along the water. [7] On one such stream, called *la crique au Sable* or Sandy Creek, they built a *gristmill* and a distillery for making alcohol. There was also a baker to supply bread in exchange for a percentage of flour that each settler had ground at the mill.

In the meantime, the Indian Wars in Ohio had reached a crisis with "Mad" Anthony Wayne's defeat of Little Turtle's warriors at the Battle of Fallen Timbers in 1794. Many of the local *habitants* used their influence with the Indians to encourage them to make peace and to sign the Treaty of Greenville. When the treaty was signed in 1795, Jean-Baptiste Sanscrainte and "Jocko" Jacques Lasselle acted as translators for the Indians, while Francois Navarre, Jean-Baptiste Couture, and several other River Raisin men signed as witnesses.

In the summer of 1796, the *habitants* were greeted by a strange new sight as the first American flag was raised over their village on the Raisin. The U.S. army built a small fort, called the Wayne Stockade, on the north bank of the river, and the *habitants* were given a choice of becoming American citizens or moving to Canada where the British were still in control. Almost all chose to stay.

Although they were now recognized as citizens, not much really changed in people's daily lives. They still depended largely on the fur trade to make a living, since markets for their farm goods were few and far away. A number of Yankee merchants and farmers arrived, but not enough to change the character of the settlement, which the Americans soon began to call "Frenchtown."

Michigan Territory was established in 1805, with William Hull as Territorial Governor and Indian Agent. By that time, there were upwards of 120 ribbon farms hugging the banks of the River Raisin, while another 40 or so were concentrated to the south on Otter Creek and to the north on Sandy Creek.

Governor Hull quickly established a militia in which he enrolled every male *habitant* between the ages of 16 and 50, adding those over 50 into a special category of their own. The 1st Michigan Regiment was based in Detroit; the 2nd Regiment, in the River Raisin Country. John Anderson, a local trader, was appointed Colonel to command the 2nd Regiment. Francois Navarre was made second in command, with the rank of Lieutenant Colonel.

The freedom-loving *habitants* disliked military discipline and thought it unfair when they were ordered to make their own uniforms from cloth which had to be purchased from Governor Hull. Fortunately, their only duty was to practice drill on certain Sundays. All in all, they were satisfied with their new lives as Americans.

This was not the case for the Potawatomies, however. In 1807, they signed a "Treaty of Friendship" with Governor Hull, in which they gave up title to all their River Raisin lands, except for the 3-square-mile Macon Reserve, some 14 miles upstream from the mouth of the river. Discontented with the loss of their lands, some began to slip away, lured to Fort Malden by British presents. Others traveled to Tippecanoe, Indiana, where the Prophet, and his brother, Tecumseh, were urging all Indians to unite in a struggle to preserve their lands and their way of life.

In November of 1811, Francois Navarre's cousin, Peter Navarre, arrived with startling news. He, along with Jean-Baptiste Sanscrainte, had been trading for furs in Tecumseh's village at Tippecanoe when a battle broke out between the Indians and some soldiers commanded by Indiana Governor William Henry Harrison. The Indians scattered and abandoned their village. The two *habitants* were afraid the soldiers would accuse them of being white renegades, so they also fled.

The news was greeted with fear and apprehension by the *habitants* of the River Raisin. It looked like war was coming with the Indians, and possibly with the British. If the British and Indians joined forces to fight the Americans, the whole frontier could go up in flames.

The American Revolution had secured the United States' independence from Great Britain, but had not brought the diplomatic respect or economic stability which the growing nation desired. The efforts of Great Britain to control American expansion and trade led to increasing tensions between the two. So began the move toward war.

There were several causes for the War of 1812, including British restrictions on trade with Napoleonic Europe, impressment of American citizens into the British navy, and Britain's support of native resistance to American settlement of the Great Lakes region. American attempts to get their way by economic coercion failed, while British efforts at compromise were too little and too late to change the course of events.

The "War Hawks", a group of young republicans from southern and western states, argued that peaceful measures had failed. Although opposed by representatives of the New England states, they pressed for war against Great Britain. One man in particular who was instrumental in the push toward war was Henry Clay. A politician from Kentucky, Clay used his position to influence the men of his state to join the fight against the British. When the Unites States government called for an increase in military forces, Kentucky raised 5000 troops when only one fifth that many were required. Although the British violations on the oceans had little direct impact on the communities of the "War Hawks", they argued that America was a sovereign nation based on an expansionist republic. It was their duty to rid the continent of the oppressive attitudes of the British once and for all. A victory against Great Britain would enable America to finally settle the maritime and commercial issues that existed between the two countries.

The most likely target to attack would be the British colony of Canada. With the British engaged in fighting Napoleon's armies in Europe, they would be unable to send much in the way of reinforcements. Thinly populated, Canada's exposed border could be crossed easily, without fear of interference by the mighty British navy.

The presence of the British forces in Canada had a somewhat different effect upon the settlers along the River Raisin, Sandy Creek, and LaPlaisance Bay. Many of the early *habitants* of these settlements originated from Canada. An invasion would be a war between "cousins," dividing families and disrupting business relationships.

Moreover, British policy considered people born in Canada to be British subjects, regardless of any later change in citizenship. Many *habitants* could thus be treated as traitors if they fought for the United States.

In addition, British relationships with the local Indians bore a certain amount of concern for those settlers who traded and lived in peace with the Potawatomi, Ottawa, Wyandotte, and other nearby Indians.

The declaration of war in June of 1812 changed life for these people forever. The atrocities of the Battles at the River Raisin would alter the structure of life within the settlements that would eventually make up Monroe County.

Genevieve & Alexis LeBeau
by Rachel Wilkie

Genevieve and Alexis LeBeau
Early Morning, July 2, 1813, at Sandy Creek

"Alexis," she called as she walked into the house. She paused a moment to let her eyes adjust to the darkness of the room. As her eyes adjusted, she walked to the wooden table her father had made for her mother as a wedding present, and carefully removed the eggs from her apron. Overhead she heard a moan followed by a thump. She smiled to herself and directed her voice toward the loft.

"Are you going to get moving? You need to help Papa with the *charette* when he gets back."

A series of clumps and thuds preceded young Alexis, only 8 years old, as he dressed for the day. Finally appearing feet first from the loft, he slowly, sleepily, began his descent. His dark brown hair was standing on end this way and that, as he rubbed the sleep from his deep brown eyes.

"It's barely light outside, 'Vieve," he complained.

"I know you are tired," she replied, "but we have so much to do to get ready."

The *habitants* living in the settlement of Sandy Creek, located about 2 miles north of the River Raisin, had been feeling many of the same tensions as the settlement of Frenchtown. Genevieve, now 13 years old was only a child when Michigan had become a Territory in 1805. She knew little of the British who had occupied the area during and after the American Revolution. Her father had told her many stories of the soldiers who were preparing to go to war against England once again. Governor William Hull was the American Governor of the Michigan Territory, but she had not yet seen the man himself. Rumors stated that he was a difficult man who made many demands on the new French-Americans.

Her thoughts were interrupted by the movements of her younger brother. Once up and out of bed, Alexis proved to be as full of energy as any other 8-year-old. Genevieve, however, as the woman of the house, was responsible for the home, garden, and livestock. She depended upon Alexis to share her duties whenever possible.

"When will father be back from the River Raisin?" Alexis asked.

"He left early so he could find Colonel Anderson at the trading post. Father was afraid he would miss him if he waited until sunrise," she answered. "Now, quickly get your hands and face washed and tend to the animals before he gets back."

The sun filtered through the thin glass panes of the window next to the washbasin. Alexis peered out into the yard as he absent-mindedly washed. His thoughts wandered to the night before when he and Genevieve sat by the fire while their father, René, and their brother-in-law Baptiste Soleau sat at the table. It had been difficult for Alexis to pay attention to his sister's instruction as she crudely taught him his English lessons.

Genevieve was fortunate to have been instructed by her older sister, Marie-Joseph, who had been included in a small group of girls who received instruction from the priest[8] when he was present at *Saint Antoine à la Rivière aux Raisins.* Alexis knew the importance of English. His papa had explained on several occasions how the world was changing and how important English would be in dealing with government officials and eastern businessmen.

Still, he had wanted desperately to listen to what the men were talking about. He had heard some of the conversation, but knew he was not supposed to listen. At one point, when it was his turn at new words, his sister had managed to catch him listening to the conversation of her

11

father. She had quickly tapped his foot and shot him a glance of warning. Shrugging his shoulders, he had reluctantly recited the new words. At this point, he had lost all track of the conversation which was becoming heated at the table.

"Vieve," he started as he dried his hands on a nearly thread-bare linen next to the washbasin, "Why was Papa so upset with Baptiste last night?"

"You weren't supposed to be listening to them talk Alexis. You know how Papa feels about us learning to speak English."

Then her face softened as she turned to her younger brother, "He wasn't upset with him. They were talking about the Americans and what was happening to our settlement and the settlement at the River Raisin."

"Oh," he answered. "Then why did they sound so angry?"

"I don't think they were angry, just concerned, " she added.

"Concerned about what?"

"If I tell you what I overheard as I was washing the supper dishes, will you get outside and start your chores?"

"Yes. Tell me!" he said eagerly.

"Well, it seems that Baptiste heard from *M'sieur* Francois Gandon that the Americans are going to fight with the British again."

"Oh," he replied, not fully understanding what this meant to him. Before he could utter another word, the sound of a horse and cart ended the conversation.

"There now," Genevieve began. "Papa is back. Go help him unload the cart."

Their father, René, walked along side of the shaggy French pony and skillfully steered it along the dirt path toward the cabin. Although the French two-wheeled cart, known to the French as a *charette*, was a convenience, there was always the threat of overturning from a tree root or rut, which would spill the contents along the path. Still, the cart was able to navigate muddy paths that were nearly impassable by foot, and René drove it often to the gristmill, hauling the family's grain. There the grain was ground into flour which he could then take over to Guyor's to have it baked into bread for supplies and trade.

Alexis raced into the yard and up to the still moving *charette*. His face beamed as he encountered his Papa for the first time that day.

"Bonjour, Papa," he sang.

"Up with the sun are you Alexis?" his father teased.

"Vieve hauled me out of bed hours ago."

"Did she now?" his father continued with a mock look of concern on his face. "Well, we have a lot of work to do today, *mon petit."*

René LeBeau reached into the pony cart, grasped a sack, then turned and gave his son an affectionate pat on the head. "Here now, give me a hand with the pony. She needs a good drink after that *voyage*."

Alexis started to unbridle the pony then paused and looked at this father. "Are the Americans going to fight the British?" he asked.

René looked at his son and sighed. He knew he would have to tell his dear children of the events unfolding around them. Yet, he wanted desperately to keep them from the unsettling news. He decided he would sit them down after the noon meal and explain what he could to them. "Tend to the pony, Alexis," he stated.

With that, Alexis knew not to push the matter. He quietly led the horse to the water trough as his father unloaded supplies.

Etienne LeBeau
by Lynn Reaume

News of the War
Late Morning, July 2, 1813

As promised, René LeBeau shared with great concern the news of a movement toward war against Great Britain with his children. He knew they needed to prepare themselves for the hardships of war, which could affect all of their lives. Still, they had been through so much, since Elizabeth, their mother, had died when the boy was just an infant. He knew all their trials had made them strong. He would break the news to them as gently as possible.

The sun was high overhead as René walked through the door, stooping so he wouldn't knock his head on the doorframe. René had built the cabin to complement his above average height, but construction of a 7-foot door to accommodate his six foot seven inches[9] was not practical. His form filled the doorway as he entered and hung his straw hat on the wall. He splashed his face with water from the basin, as was his habit whenever he came in from tending to the morning work around the farm.

Genevieve had cleared all evidence of the morning meal, and was dutifully setting things right for their weekly trip to the River Raisin settlement. She could feel his gaze as she busied herself with her duties. Turning to face him, she noticed a slight frown on her Papa's face. "He looks old when he frowns that way," she thought.

As if in answer to her unasked question he summoned the children to his side. "You are curious about the happenings within the settlements," he began. "I had tried to keep the news from you, then realized that all that is happening may well affect you both."

"We aren't babies, Papa," Genevieve defended. "Well at least I'm not." She shot her brother a glance. Alexis had been busy replacing firewood at the hearth for

Genevieve when his father came in the room. Now all his attention was focused on René's face.

"Tell us please, Papa," Alexis begged. *"S'il te plaît."*

"When I passed through Frenchtown this morning, on my way to Anderson's trading post, the place was alive with rumors. I asked the Colonel myself what the noise was about. He told me that early in the morning a Captain Fowler came galloping in on horseback with an urgent dispatch from General Hull. It seems the General had just received word that war had been declared against the British." René paused briefly as his children's mouths hung agape. He continued, "General Hull sent Fowler to get information about the Cuyahoga[10] which sailed for Detroit before the news of the declaration reached the General. He wanted us to send a boat out to warn the Cuyahoga, but I'm afraid it may be too late to catch the ship before it comes within range of the British guns at Fort Malden.

Even as I stood there the sound of a column of men could be heard approaching. Captain LaCroix had collected about 150 men and several teams of oxen and was heading towards the road to continue their work. Anderson ran off to get his axe. He said he would work alongside the militiamen and encourage them as much as possible. Without the work being done on the road Hull will not be able to get his supply wagons through to Detroit. They're big, heavy, monstrous wagons, not like our agile charette. I was also sent with word for your brother, Etienne to get his axe and head for the Raisin. He will help build the road."

"How is it then that you acquired the goods you unloaded with all the commotion around?" Genevieve asked.

"Mrs. Anderson kindly took my order, but was reluctant to part with too much. She said her first order of business was to supply the militia as much as her husband would allow. Anderson is supplying the troops with axes from his own stores, since none of the ones he ordered from the army command in Detroit have arrived.

We have traded for many years at Frenchtown. Besides, the men of Sandy Creek are being called to serve the army," concluded René.

Silence filled the room as the information washed across the young minds.

Soldiers of the Frontier Army
by Joe Lee

A Visit to the Raisin
Late Afternoon, July 2, 1813

Etienne, the oldest son of René LeBeau, was now in service in Hubert LaCroix's Company of Major James Witherell's Battalion of Michigan Volunteers. His younger brother, Alexis, was especially excited at the prospect of seeing the American army in all their finery. René told his younger children that they would travel to the River Raisin and watch the militia officially called to muster as the American army passed through the settlement.[11] Marie, his oldest daughter, and her husband, Baptiste, would join them at the home of Margaret and Etienne Couture, René's second daughter and her husband, along the banks of the Raisin.

As the LeBeau family arrived at the River Raisin, Margaret Couture met them outside her home.

Genevieve smiled as she caught sight of her older sister. Although they lived only two and a half miles from one another, visits were infrequent during the summer due to the amount of work that each day brought. The warm months in the Great Lakes region were important for their survival during the winter months. Food was grown, harvested and dried or preserved for the long winter months ahead.

"It's good to see you again, Margaret," Genevieve began. "Alexis, hand down the basket so I can show Margaret what I brought along for the day."

Genevieve turned to retrieve the basket from her brother. She quickly uncovered the contents to show her sister. "I've got enough to feed all of us tonight."

The basket held a dish she had prepared, which fortunately had the ability to travel well. The recipe was her mother's and had been handed down from her mother, who learned it from her mother and on down through the years until no one was sure where it originated.

The night before, Genevieve had hung a kettle over the fire, nearly full of water and added several quarts of peas that Alexis had picked from the garden. When the peas were nearly bursting, two pounds of pork was cut into strips and added to the peas. The kettle simmered throughout the night. When Genevieve woke, she broke and added four biscuits left from the previous evening's meal to the mixture. By the time they were ready to leave for Frenchtown, the biscuits had expanded and filled the kettle to the brim.

"I hope your cooking has improved since I left home," Margaret teased as she put an arm around her younger sister. Together they walked toward the cabin, anxious to tell each other the latest news.

While the women retreated, Alexis jumped from the pony *charette* and led the animal to water so it could rest. René turned and helped Marie, who had arrived shortly after them with Baptiste, from their *charette*. Her arms were filled with additional supplies for the day. She followed the path her sisters had taken to the house leaving the men to stretch their legs after the journey.

"It is good to see you, *Mon Vieux*," a voice sounded from the east of the farm.

René looked for the source, knowing well who referred to him in such a familiar manner. Seeing Etienne Couture, René shook his head amused with the young man's lack of respect. "How can you speak to your guest in such a way?" René teased. "Why we could just as easily pass your home as stop!"

As Etienne approached the men, he extended his hand in a gesture of surrender. Etienne was wearing the official uniform of the local militia, which had been organized by General Hull as the 2nd Michigan Territorial

Militia Regiment. His wife, Margaret, had sewn it from the prescribed blue cloth purchased at great expense from General Hull himself. It was trimmed in white to distinguish the 2nd Regiment from the red-trimmed uniform of the 1st Michigan in Detroit.

"René, Baptiste, I am glad you are here. Please, accept my most humble apologies. Sometimes my sarcastic tongue gets the best of me," he continued with a smile playing on his lips.

René knew that Etienne was not the least bit sorry, but his sense of humor was refreshing. It seemed that everything these days was serious; war, Indian attacks, and the arrival of the American army. Etienne Couture's humor was welcome. René had admired the young man for it as soon as he met him. He found it refreshing that a young man could be serious, hard working and amusing. Margaret was pleased with his demeanor as well.

"You are taking care of my daughter I trust," René replied, not eager to address the reason for the visit.

"Of course, *Mon Vieux,*" Etienne replied. "At least as much as I am able with the settlement in such a panic since the news of the war."

Smiles dropped from the faces of the men as they collectively thought of the recent changes to their lives.

"Well, I for one will be relieved when the Americans run the British off the continent. I've had more than enough with the King's promoting the Indian uprisings," Baptiste announced.

René looked to his son-in-law with a frown. If Etienne had a sarcastic tongue, then Baptiste surely had a sharper one. LeBeau had a great deal of respect for Soleau, but he had spent enough time with him to know that his pointed comments sometimes led him to trouble. "We will all be relieved to have the British leave, Baptiste, but what concerns me is the price we will have to pay for it."

"With all due respect, Sir . . ." Baptiste was cut off by the approach of young Alexis. He ran excitedly toward the trio, stopping short just before he ran into Etienne.

"What has you so excited, lad?" René began.

"The soldiers are coming from the south," he gasped, "Hurry, Papa! We have to see them call out the militia!"

"Easy, *mon fils*," René soothed. "We have plenty of time before they reach the River Raisin. After all, Etienne could not stand here talking to us if the call had gone out."

René turned to Etienne and raised his eyebrows in question. "Shouldn't you join the ranks, son?" he asked.

"I was on my way when you arrived. I have only to stop and bid good-bye to Margaret," he answered. Removing his round hat, Etienne Couture walked to the house and disappeared inside the door.

Alexis was hardly able to contain his excitement as the American army marched before him. He stared wide-eyed at the troops as he bounced on his heels scanning the men for his older brother, Etienne. Genevieve placed her hand on the bobbing form beside her in an attempt to settle his enthusiasm.

Alexis turned his face away from the parade only long enough to ask his father, René, if he knew where Etienne was in the ranks. René explained that Captain LaCroix's company had already left for the Huron River to build a bridge for the army to cross.

Alexis, somewhat disappointed by his father's statement, quickly recovered as his attention was then drawn to the large, proud figure riding in front of the approaching American army. General Hull made an imposing sight despite the brown drizzle of chewing tobacco which stained the corner of his mouth.

Behind him marched Colonel Miller and his regulars of the 4th U.S. Infantry. They were resplendent in dark blue uniforms and wore tall, stove-pipe hats called shakos. Following the regulars came three battalions of Ohio militia, rough, undisciplined frontier troops dressed in gray hunting shirts, with huge knives stuck in their leather belts.

The General gave the command for the army to halt. The crowd grew silent as the commander of the army prepared to address them. He began, "The army will march to Detroit in the morning. We expect to be met at the River Huron by Tecumseh with many Indians. The British have taken several American vessels with supplies for this army. I need not tell you, that every exertion will be made for the safety of this country, and the honor of the American arms." The crowd cheered as General Hull commanded the troops to wheel about and march off toward their camp.

Militiaman from the River Raisin, Summer, 1812
by Joe Lee

Returning Home
Sandy Creek, August 11, 1812

Days passed slowly for the LeBeau family with no word from Etienne. Since the American army left Frenchtown for Detroit, Indians from outside the area were seen more frequently at the Sandy Creek settlement. The once friendly encounters between the French and Indians gave way to tensions and sometimes even fear. Alexis noticed that his Potawatomi playmates didn't come to the settlement anymore. By the beginning of August, René had heard that the Native warriors led by Chief Tecumseh had cut the American supply road between Detroit and Frenchtown. Supplies could get no further than the River Raisin.

Genevieve stooped in the small garden near the cabin. She had planted corn, peas, onions, squash, and other vegetables which could be stored for the winter. As she gathered the last of the beans, she glanced up and wiped her brow. The sun was setting but was still high enough to outline a form approaching on horseback. She squinted into the sun, and realized the familiar form was that of her brother, Etienne LeBeau.

"Etienne! Etienne!" Genevieve called. "Where have you been? *Qu'est-ce qui est arrivé?* What's happened to you? We've been so worried."

Etienne was shorter than his father René, but still stood almost a foot above his sister Genevieve. Atop his horse, he was a sight to behold. His dark brown hair was curly like that of Alexis'. He had inherited most of his physical attributes from the LeBeau side of the family. Genevieve, however, was petit with long straight hair. She had auburn highlights, which shone in the evening sun as she welcomed her brother home.

"I'm alright," Etienne told her. "Had a close call though. Captain LaCroix[12] sent 25 of us to Detroit. We reached the American army on its way here, but then got ambushed at Brownstown. The Ohio militia retreated all the way to Detroit leaving dead bodies scattered all along the road."

"But you're not hurt, are you?" she asked with a worried look on her face.

"No, like I said, I'm fine," he assured her. "But my *canteen* got smashed by a bullet. Claude Couture lost his horse and James Knaggs' face was scarred. But Louis Jacob was the only one who was hurt bad. They took him to see Dr. Austin at the Wayne Stockade then over to Doctor Dazette's."[13]

"Come down from that horse and inside," Genevieve scolded, as if she were his mother. "Alexis! Lexi?" she shouted across the yard.

From around the corner of the house Alexis came running. He stopped short at the sight of his brother.

"Tend to the horse, Alexis, and fetch Papa from the field. Tell him Etienne is home," Genevieve ordered. She then followed her older brother into the safety of their home.

Chief Tecumseh
from Bulkley's "History of Monroe County"

Surrender and Occupation
Sandy Creek, August 11, 1812

The Battle of Brownstown was one of three attempts to clear the supply road to Detroit. This battle was soon followed by the Battle of Monguagon. The Americans were unsuccessful at opening the route, and most of the army remained at Detroit until a large force of British led by General Isaac Brock crossed the Detroit River from Fort Malden in Canada. Feeling resistance was futile, General Hull surrendered the city without a fight. The militia of Sandy Creek and the River Raisin were sent home on parole. Although the war would go on, those men were not supposed to take part in it.[14]

René sat next to the hearth nodding in the amber glow of the sunset. Genevieve had cooked a chicken with corn chowder for the evening's meal. Fighting the urge to sleep, René turned his thoughts to the recent events at the settlement. The surrender of the Americans was a disappointment. Still he felt relieved that neither his son, Etienne, or his son-in-law Etienne Couture had been injured.[15] His thoughts were interrupted by a loud knock.

Opening the door, René was surprised to see the familiar face of his neighbor, Francois Gandon. "Bonjour," he said, motioning his friend inside. Gandon appeared to be excited about something. He removed his hat to wipe the sweat from his brow, revealing his unusually blond hair. "What's the matter?" asked René.

"I thought my time had come," Gandon relied. "Two Delaware and a couple of Ottawas stopped by my place. They accused me of being one of the *American Long Knives*, because of my blond hair, and threatened to kill me."

"You're lucky they didn't. Since our Etienne returned, and after Colonel Anderson surrendered our militia to the British, there have been a lot of problems with the Indians. It is especially those from far away who don't know how well we get along with the local Potawatomies."

"These Indians really weren't after me," continued Gandon. "They were out to get Colonel Anderson. They said he was a cheat and a liar. One of them stuck his knife in my floor and said he was going to cut off Anderson's hands and cut out his tongue so he couldn't write or talk to the Americans. I sent my young boarder to the River Raisin to warn Anderson to get out of town. The British officers don't seem to be able to control their Indian allies, or maybe they just don't want to. I hope they will listen to their chief, Tecumseh."

"*Oui*," said René. "Tecumseh is a good man. He will know how to keep them in line."

Tecumseh was in fact a good man. On several occasions he intervened between settlers and other Indians. With the tension mounting at the Sandy Creek settlement, René LeBeau made frequent trips to the River Raisin. On one such occasion, Genevieve and Alexis went with him.

Upon their arrival at Frenchtown, the LeBeaus came upon a small gathering of people.

"Papa," Genevieve asked. "What do you suppose is happening?"

"Why don't we see?" he answered.

Tecumseh had called a council meeting and was making a speech. The LeBeaus had no sooner come in sight of the Indian than a little girl approached the chief. The child tugged at the fringe of Tecumseh's hunting shirt. The chief looked down and smiled at the little girl, but continued speaking. The girl tugged again and Tecumseh listened.

"Come to our house," she said. "Some bad Indians are at our house."

There was some confusion in front of Genevieve, but as the crowd parted, she realized that Tecumseh had stopped speaking. She saw the Shawnee Chief turn and walk away at a fast pace with the girl skipping behind him. Eventually he stopped at a house, the home of Mrs. Ruland. As he and the girl approached the front door, they encountered two or three Wyandotte Indians dragging out a trunk.

Tecumseh was visibly angry. He grabbed his silver-mounted tomahawk and swung it at the nearest warrior, stopping him in his tracks. The other Wyandottes rushed to help their comrade, but stopped short when the chief exclaimed, "Dogs! I am Tecumseh!"

Without a word of protest, the three Wyandots rushed out the door. Just then, Tecumseh noticed some British soldiers in the house. He turned to them and stated angrily, "you are worse than dogs!"

A guard was offered to Mrs. Ruland by the soldiers but she refused. Pointing her finger at Tecumseh, her reply was, "No. So long as that man is around, we feel safe."[16]

New Year's Fiddler
by Lynn Reaume

The Holidays
December, 1812 – January, 1813

The settlements of Sandy Creek and the River Raisin remained under British control through the fall of 1812. Frequent appearances of British, Indians, and Canadian militia worried the French settlers, but even under the shadow of the war the LeBeaus held fast to family traditions through the holiday season.

At Christmas time, many of the *habitants* traveled to Detroit to visit with relatives and attend mass at St. Anne's Church. Yet others in the area of occupation remained close to home, even though St. Antoine's Church did not have a resident priest at this time. The local custom was to share an evening meal with family, sing carols such as *"D'où viens-tu, bergère?"* or "Whence, O Shepherd?"

René brought his children to the house of his son–in–law, Etienne Couture, for Christmas dinner. Margaret, Marie-Joseph, and Genevieve cooked and served, while the men and Alexis talked about the state of their settlements. The events of the past months were enough to cast a bleak shadow over the family, but each and every person present was thankful that everyone was safe and healthy.

René offered a prayer and a toast as they were seated around the table for the meal. He thanked the Heavenly Father for bringing his family together to worship and remember Jesus' birth and added, "If you can't give us more happiness than you have in the past year, please don't give us any less."[17]

The early morning hours of Christmas were quiet and white as René drove his two sons and daughter back to their home on Sandy Creek. The brisk wind kept Alexis from sleeping even while he was snuggly wrapped in his capote. The sleigh René used was similar to his pony cart with wooden blades on the underside of the main frame instead of wheels. The passengers bobbed across the snow-covered ground anticipating the warmth of the fire they would start at home. The only sounds came from the sliding of the sleigh, the wind blowing in the trees, and Alexis' repeated claim that he was not tired each time his head nodded in sleep.

Genevieve, however, fully admitted her fatigue. She had risen early to prepare for the day at the River Raisin. Since the occupation, it had been difficult for the French to get necessary items such as cloth and buttons. However, Genevieve had set her mind to having a new set of clothing prepared for her father, brothers, and herself by Christmas. Her garden had yielded extra food this harvest, and she used the excess in trade for cloth. She had sent Etienne once to Detroit with dried vegetables. He had returned with only a few yards of gray wool. Next she sent him with bags of dried apples and pears from their own trees. These were welcomed by the tailor Charles LaFleur, and he gladly exchanged several yards of cloth for them.

Genevieve spent many evenings cutting, sewing and adding finishing touches to the garments. She did not end up with complete outfits for each, but the additions were greatly needed and appreciated. Alexis had commented on the loose fit of his new capote. "It practically drags the ground," he protested.

Genevieve smiled as she thought of her brother snuggled deep inside the oversized coat. "He certainly isn't complaining now," she thought.

The observation of Christmas was mainly a religious holiday for the French. New Year's Eve, however, was considered a festive time in which people joined together in celebration with family, friends and neighbors.

It was on the morning of January 1, 1813, that Genevieve awoke early and climbed down from the loft to rekindle the fire. She considered using the Yule log first lit at Christmas, then decided to save it for the arrival of her sisters later that day.

As the flames sprang to life, her thoughts wandered back to the night before. René was telling stories about the New Year's Eves he remembered from his childhood, when he was interrupted by shouts and laughter and a loud knocking at the door. Alexis opened the door and in came at least a dozen strangely dressed people. His eyes grew wide as the stream of people filled the room. René smiled at his son's reaction as the gang of people broke into song:

"Give us food for the poor," they chanted to the tune of a fiddle. "some meat or corn or we'll take your daughter instead."[18]   One of the larger men grabbed Genevieve's arm and whirled her out the door. The mob followed out the door with Alexis behind. Before they had reached the garden fence, René gave in, offering a small sack of dried peas and a bottle of wine. Genevieve remembered the hesitation of her partner as he considered her father's offer. Then as quickly as she had been swept away, she was released and left standing, breathless, outdoors in her *chemise*.

She knew it had been all in fun, as it was every year, but with all the excitement it took her a great deal of time to calm Alexis enough for bed.

Her thoughts were interrupted as a sound came from above her head. She turned her face toward the loft as another noise sounded from above. Even the excitement of last night couldn't keep Alexis in bed today, she thought.

January first brought the promise of a new year. She hoped that the war would come to an end soon, and life would return to normal. As with Christmas, the LeBeaus would usher in the New Year with the same traditions they shared with generations of French before them.

Genevieve climbed halfway up the ladder and peered into the loft. Alexis was just sitting up on the small framed feather bed at the far corner of the room. He rubbed his eyes and let out a sigh. "Vieve?" he asked.

"Yes, Lexi," she soothed. "Let's go wake Papa." It was traditional that on New Years Day all children, whether living at home or married, knelt at their father's feet, as soon as they saw him, for his blessing. The LeBeau children had followed this tradition ever since they could remember.

Together, Genevieve and Alexis made their way to René's bedside. Genevieve could tell by the peaceful smile on her father's lips that he was awake, but was waiting for them to come in before he got out of bed. Carefully opening one eye, René peeked at his children as they knelt beside him. He decided to play possum for a few seconds while they studied his motionless figure. Alexis leaned over to his sister to whisper when René sat straight up in bed, giving them both a start. He laughed a full, round laugh and held out his arms for his children to come closer.

René placed wet, rough kisses on the cheeks of Alexis and Genevieve then motioned for them to take their former positions at the side of his bed. He then offered his blessing to each child by placing his hand on their bowed heads, made the sign of the cross, and offered a short prayer.

Today the rest of the LeBeau family would gather at René's home. The women would prepare *tourtières* and fruit pies for the family dinner. Gifts would be exchanged between adults and the children. It would be a festive event for all, a pleasant diversion for all the residents of Sandy Creek and the River Raisin.

René LeBeau & Genevieve
by Joe Lee

LeBeau House
January 18, 1813

Increased snowfall at Sandy Creek kept the members of the LeBeau family mostly indoors. Alexis and Etienne completed their morning rituals of feeding and watering the animals. As they finished and were returning to the house, Etienne saw his brother-in-law, Baptiste Soleau approaching. Etienne waited at the end of the foot-path for him.

"What brings you out on a morning like this?" Etienne asked.

"Is your father inside? Come. I've just received news from the Raisin," Baptiste replied.

The two men went into the house and found René at the hearth, drinking cider. Genevieve looked up from her mending as they entered. René stood and greeted his son-in-law with a hearty handshake.

"René," Baptiste began. "I need to discuss a matter with you and Etienne." His eyes strayed to Alexis who was removing his capote near the door.

René looked to his young son, then nodded to Baptiste. "Alexis?" René began. "I need you to go out and help your sister gather the eggs."

Alexis sighed and put his capote back on. Genevieve was aware of the three men watching as she put away her mending to join Alexis. The men were waiting for the younger LeBeaus to leave the room so they could talk. "Come, Lexi," she said as she made her way out the door.

Shutting the heavy door behind them, Genevieve stopped and listened. Her little brother said, "Come on Vieve," but she shushed him and pulled him closer as the men's voices from inside became louder.

"Listen," she said, as the tone of the voices changed. It appeared they were almost arguing. The children heard their father René's voice saying, "No, you can't go."

"René," Baptiste tried to reason. "Word has come from Charland[19] that 600 Kentuckians[20] are coming to help rid the settlement of the Canadians and Indians. He wants all available men to grab their guns and meet on the ice at LaPlaisance Bay."[21]

"I'm well aware that it is a serious situation, but Etienne has served his time in the militia and made it back safely. I don't want him to risk himself again," René argued.

"I have a duty to join those men, Papa," Etienne argued back. "We are not fighting for the Americans, but to save our settlement. The British have taken most of our supplies and will surely burn our homes to the ground just like they did to Alexis Soleau's gristmill. Since Tecumseh has left on a visit to the southern tribes, nobody will be able to control the Indians."

René sighed. "There are enough Kentucky soldiers to defeat the British and all of their Indian allies. Why do you insist on joining the fight? Last August when Colonel Anderson[22] surrendered the militia and Frenchtown you were put on parole. You promised not to fight against the British anymore. If you are caught fighting this time they will kill you for breaking your parole."

Baptiste placed his hand on his father-in-law's shoulder. "We will be here at Sandy Creek to protect our families, René."

Etienne looked at his father then to Jean-Baptiste and stated, "I'm going." He turned and gathered his gun and coat. René watched in silent disapproval as his son paused near the door. René could not deter Etienne from going. He wondered if he would ever see his son again.

Etienne paused in front of the closed door. Baptiste walked to him and offered his support with a nod. As Etienne opened the door, Genevieve and Alexis rushed in, near to tears. "You can't go, Etienne," Genevieve sobbed.

Etienne placed a kiss on the top of his sister's head. "Take care of Alexis. Don't worry. All will be well," he assured her. He left his family watching silently from the doorway, as he set off for the River Raisin.

At the First Battle of the River Raisin
by Joe Lee

Battle of River Raisin
January 18, 1813

It was almost three o'clock before Etienne joined the small group of militiamen who gathered on the open prairie south of the River Raisin. They were mostly from the little settlements at Otter Creek and LaPlaisance Bay, but more of the River Raisin men were arriving at every moment.

To the north, a quarter mile away, on the other side of the frozen river, the whitewashed houses of Frenchtown glistened in the afternoon sunlight. Behind the picket fences, there was a flurry of activity as Major Ebenezer Reynolds, the British commander, positioned several hundred Canadians and Indians to defend the village from the American assault he knew was about to come.

Off to his right Etienne could see the American army, over 600 Kentuckians, drawn up in battle formation. In front of them was their commander, Lt. Colonel William Lewis. He was addressing his troops. Etienne could make out most of the English words as he spoke:

"Soldiers! Your ancient enemy is before you. The wrongs that he has inflicted upon your country are fresh in your memory. That country calls upon you this day to vindicate her honor and her interests by inflicting upon him condign punishment. In the hour of battle, remember what the Patriot Orator said to you at Georgetown, you have the double character of Americans and Kentuckians to sustain! Do so, as I feel assured you will, and all will be well."

The Kentucky soldiers broke their silence and cheered as Lewis completed his speech. Their loud *Huzzahs* were stopped short, however, as a cannonball flew over their heads.

Etienne turned away from the shot and declared, "Don't worry, that British cannon is about big enough to kill a mouse!" As the second shot passed overheard, the Kentucky troops began crowing like roosters and barking like dogs. Orders were given to advance without delay. Seeing the American line advancing, Captain Ambrose Charland, appointed commander of the locals, gave the word and the citizen soldiers joined the attack.

As they approached the river, there was a third cannon shot, but nobody was hurt. Seized with determination to take their town back from the enemy, the French militiamen broke into a run, passing the Kentuckians and clambering down onto the slippery river ice.

As they reached the opposite bank, the men instinctively paused and began peppering the enemy positions with *musket balls and buckshot*. They were soon joined by Captain Bland Ballard[23] and his advance guard of Kentucky militiamen, who re-formed their ranks and began firing *volleys* at the British.

As the smoke cleared, Etienne looked towards the river, where he could see the Kentuckians helping one of their officers, a Captain Paschal Hickman.[24] He had fallen from the saddle when his horse stumbled and broke through the thin ice at the edge of the riverbank. Fortunately the water at this point was only a few inches deep, but the unfortunate captain was then hit in the leg by a musket ball while trying to remount his horse.

The main American line had now come up, led by Colonel Lewis and Majors Graves and Madison[25]. Although enemy bullets were still falling like hail all around them, Etienne could hear the Kentucky drummer begin to sound the long roll. This was a signal for a general charge. The French and Kentuckians went forward in a rush, climbing over the picket fences and swarming around the buildings. Still firing, the enemy abandoned the village and retreated towards the safety of the woods a half mile away.

Etienne approached one of the buildings and saw a familiar figure waving at him from a window. It was his in-law, 48-year-old Jean-Baptiste Couture. Etienne suddenly thought of his sister, Margaret, who had married Jean-Baptiste's brother, Etienne Couture.

"Is my sister in the village?" he asked.

"Don't worry, she's safe," answered Couture. "My brother took her and the rest of our family to Colonel Navarre's house earlier today, when we heard the American army was coming to liberate Frenchtown."

"So, why didn't you go with them, *mon vieux?*" asked Etienne.

"Are you crazy?" Couture shouted back. "I'll be hanged if I abandon my property to such a gang of thieves! They must have half the food supply in the settlement gathered up in Jerome's[26] barn, waiting to be shipped off to the British base at Fort Malden. You wait right where you are. I have a musket hidden upstairs. I'll get it and together, we'll chase these rascals out of our settlement."

As he waited in front of Couture's house, Etienne could see the American right flank, out on the open ground. There, Colonel Allen[27] and his men had been forced back by heavy enemy fire. Now, however, with the forces under Colonel Lewis advancing beyond the fences of Frenchtown, Colonel Allen again led his men forward.

When Couture came out, the two headed off towards the fighting, which was now going on beyond the garden fences of the settlement. They caught up with Etienne's comrades, just as Peter Navarre[28] and his two brothers were returning with an Indian prisoner in tow. They were pretty proud of themselves, as they bragged they were the only ones able to capture any of the Indians that day.

The Kentuckians were also rejoicing. In the mad dash across the river and through the village, they had killed and *scalped* a dozen Indians, while only three Kentuckians had been wounded. They had also taken two of the Canadians prisoner.

But the battle was not over. Once the British force reached the woods, the Indians and Canadians fought more stubbornly. As the Kentuckians approached, they fired from behind trees, then ducked back into the bushes and ran off before the Kentucky volunteers could react. Reaching a safe position, the Indians reloaded their muskets and waited until the Kentuckians advanced once more into view. Before this fight would end, a dozen Kentucky soldiers would die, and 55 more would be wounded.

Although not as experienced in the woods as the Indian warriors, the Kentuckians took to the trees as well, firing whenever they saw an enemy run from cover. They continued their attack until the early evening, when the winter sky began to grow black. The soldiers had been fighting well over three hours, constantly firing and advancing. Now, the darkness was making it difficult to even reload their *muskets*. As Etienne spilled more powder into his *priming pan*, he began to wonder if the battle would ever end.

One other thought was on his mind, as well. It was a very disturbing thought. As the enemy retreated, they were heading north, north towards Etienne's home on Sandy Creek, north towards where his father, sister, and little brother were waiting for his return.[29]

Death at Sandy Creek
Evening, January 18, 1813

For quite a while after Etienne left Sandy Creek, René remained in a dark mood. Baptiste Soleau returned home to secure his house and farm. Genevieve remained inside the house, but avoided her father. She knew he needed time to sort out his feelings about Etienne's departure. She quietly went about her regular duties, preparing a meal, and washing the *redware* plates and bowls. Alexis, however, was not as easily contained. For a time he sat looking out the window, then put on his capote and headed out into the snow.

As darkness descended, the sounds of battle could be heard at Sandy Creek. René silently slipped outside to get Alexis. He found his son near the garden fence, gazing off in the direction of the battle.

"Alexis," René barked. "It's not safe out here. Come inside."

"Papa?" Alexis started as he turned to follow his father back to the house. "Do you think Etienne will be safe?"

René bent on one knee in front of his young son so he could look into Alexis' eyes. Placing a finger under the boy's chin he gently answered, "I don't know." The two LeBeaus walked silently back to the warmth and safety of their house.

A short distance up-stream, Baptiste assured himself that he was right to encourage Etienne to fight with the Americans. He understood René's determination to keep his family safe. He had sent his wife, Marie-Joseph, and his children, Catherine and Baptiste to Detroit with Francois Gandon[30] and his family. Marie-Joseph was with child; she had but a month before their third would be born.

Sandy Creek was no place for them with the threat of battle and Indians slipping in and out daily. He had tried to convince René to take Genevieve and Alexis to Detroit as well. He had refused, saying that he had Etienne to help him defend his home. Now that Etienne was at battle, René and the children were left to protect themselves and their farm. He said a silent prayer as he walked, that the LeBeaus would be safe. He should have prayed for himself.

The sounds of battle rose over the woods as he approached the Gandon farm. Baptiste had promised Francois Gandon that he would do what he could to protect the family's possessions. Baptiste felt uneasy as he checked each building. He had a responsibility to his neighbor, and as long as he could hear distant gunfire, he was certain that no Indians would be passing through Sandy Creek until the fight was over.

He had passed the ruins of the burned out *gristmill* his uncle had built along the banks of Sandy Creek around dusk. It was fully dark by the time he reached Gandon's. He noticed that the sounds of musket fire were getting closer than before. When he was satisfied with his inspection, he turned for home. As the darkness grew deeper, fewer and fewer shots could be heard from the south. Eventually the night grew quiet.

As Baptiste walked, he heard noises to his left, in the woods. He paused and tried to see who was approaching. Within moments, several Native warriors came into view. Baptiste froze, wondering if this meant the Americans had been successful in defeating the British forces at Frenchtown. "Otherwise, why would the Indians be heading back through Sandy Creek?" he thought. Still, he was unsure of the days' outcome. He had to be cautious. Baptiste thought the Indians seemed in good spirits considering their experience. "Maybe," he thought, "the British were not defeated."

One of the warriors walked out of the shadows toward Baptiste. Not wanting to appear afraid, Baptiste asked in *Anishinabemowin,* the Potawatomi language, "Are you running from the Americans? The Big Knives?"

His answer came unexpectedly in the form of a flash of light and the report of a musket. Baptiste felt a searing pain in his side and he immediately staggered off into the woods in the direction of his father-in-law's cabin.

The Indian who fired the shot motioned to a couple others to follow the injured man into the woods, but they kept their distance. Baptiste kept up his pace along the path glancing every so often behind to see if he was being followed. What he saw instead of Indians, was a trail of blood from his wound. He was unsure if he was followed, but continued to the LeBeau farm where he knew he could find help.

At the LeBeau cabin, Genevieve listened to the even breathing of her brother Alexis. She knew he had finally gone to sleep. They had actually gone to bed hours ago, but her mind was racing with thoughts of Etienne and questions about what happened that day at The River Raisin. A low glow came up the ladder of the loft from the fireplace below. Genevieve knew her father was awake, still waiting for Etienne to return.

A muffled yell came from outside, but she couldn't make out what was said. Genevieve heard the scuffling of approaching footsteps. She could hear her father open the door and the voice of Baptiste crying out in pain. " *Au secours*! René, help me. I think they've killed me."

Genevieve remained silent until she heard her brother-in-law's statement, then she let out a gasp. She climbed from her bed and toward the ladder. She peered down into the room to see her father kneeling beside Baptiste who was lying on the floor. René tried to lift his son-in-law to take him to the bed, but Baptiste's body hung lifeless in his arms.

Genevieve drew a breath and tried to stop a sob beginning in her throat. She crawled to the side of Alexis' bed. As she reached his side she heard another commotion at the door. She shook Alexis to wake him. His arm flew toward her in his sleep, but she shook him more urgently until he opened his eyes.

Alexis saw his sister's face over him as he came out of his sleep. Genevieve put a finger to her lips to warn Alexis to be silent. He was about to sit up in bed when a shot rang out below. Without hesitation, Genevieve grabbed her brother and pulled him under the bed. Alexis didn't know what was happening. Genevieve knew that the shot and the sounds that followed were her father. Tears welled up in her eyes as she held Alexis still under the bed. Whoever was down there was still in the house, she could feel it. A sudden clang as if a tin was dropped made her jump, but she held fast to her brother. His eyes pleaded with her to know what was happening. She knew they couldn't speak. They lie waiting for what seemed like hours before the house once again fell silent.

Uncertain if the danger had passed, Genevieve released Alexis and slowly pulled herself from under the bed. She motioned for him to stay where he was, but he shook his head and began to crawl out of hiding.

"What . . ." Alexis tried to ask, but Genevieve's look warned him not to speak. She knew Alexis was afraid, but she still didn't know what had happened to Baptiste and most likely also to their father. She wanted to be sure no one was inside the house. She carefully peered over the loft opening, her body pressed flat against the boards. Her view was limited to a small area of the room. She could not see the door. She didn't even know if her father and Baptiste were still inside the cabin, or if they had been dragged off. Slowly she turned and descended the ladder. With each step she could see more of the room. Halfway down, she saw her father, motionless on the floor. She held her breath and her throat grew tight as she continued her descent. She could see both men lying on the floor, the door of the cabin open a crack. Confident that no one was inside, she quickly climbed the ladder to get Alexis. She found him huddled against his bed with his arms wrapped around his knees. His eyes were wide as she came to him and sat down beside him. "Lexi," she whispered. "We have to get out of the house."

"Where's Papa?" he asked. His eyes searched her face for answers.

"While you were asleep, Baptiste came to the door. He was hurt. Papa tried to help him, but whoever shot Baptiste came to our house and shot Papa too."

"No!" Alexis called out as tears streaked from his frightened eyes. Genevieve gathered him into her arms, partly to comfort him, and partly to quiet him.

"Lexi, listen to me. Whoever did this might still be here. It is almost light. We have to run."

"Where will we go?" He asked, tears still dropping from his cheeks.

"I think we should try to get to Frenchtown. Maybe we can find Etienne or Margaret. The soldiers may still be there. We will be safe once we get there. Now, Lexi, we have to be strong. Papa would want that of us. We have to be quiet when we go downstairs so we can look outside to see if anyone is out there."

Alexis nodded his head but was not at all sure if he could be strong. He wanted to crawl back in bed and cry. The two LeBeau children climbed down the ladder and stood hand-in-hand facing the door. The *embers* in the fireplace gave off enough light to show the forms of their loved ones on the floor. Alexis held tightly to Genevieve as they slowly walked past the hearth. Pausing next to their father, Genevieve released Alexis' hand and looked upon the face of her father. She knew he was no longer with them because his eyes remained open and fixed. A tear slid down her cheek as she gently placed her hand upon René LeBeau's eyes and closed his lids. She again reached for her brother's hand and stood with him saying silent prayers and good-byes to their beloved father. Baptiste's body lay near the closed door, face down on the floor. Alexis looked at the form of his brother-in-law and bowed his head.

The light of morning began to shine through the window. Genevieve gently pulled her brother's hand toward the door. From the rear of the house they heard a voice. Genevieve knew the language she heard was Potawatomi and the voice was not friendly. "We have to go now Lexi! If those Indians find us now . . ." She pulled him toward the door.

"What about my *moccasins*?" Alexis asked.

"We have no time! Those Indians must not know we are here or they would have taken us already. We have to go now or they will catch us in the house," Genevieve declared.

"I don't want to go!" Alexis cried.

"SHHH!" Genevieve whispered.

Tears began to well up in Alexis' eyes once again. He looked around the cabin that had been his home all his life. His eyes rested once again on his father. With a deep breath, Alexis faced his sister once again and said, "I'm ready. I need to be brave for Papa."

Genevieve grasped her brother's hand and stepped quietly to the door. Sounds from outside the cabin assured her that there were at least a couple of people near the house. Her thoughts raced as she tried to think of some way to escape the house without being seen. Footsteps approached from the right side of the cabin. One of the

Indians said he was going into the house to see if he could find any more valuables now that it was light. With a gasp, Genevieve knew it was now or never to flee. She gave Alexis a quick hug and looked quickly through the window. The yard was empty for the time being, but within moments the Indians would be coming through the front door. "Ready?"

Alexis nodded and took a deep breath. Genevieve flung open the door and ran out into the snow. Alexis was right beside her, but he let out a cry as his feet sank into the cold snow. His cry was enough to alert the Indians. Alexis and Genevieve ran across the field as fast as their feet would carry them. Alexis could hear shouts as he ran. The snow was cold and slippery, but he did his best to keep up with his sister. He looked back at the cabin for a second and saw two Indians shouting with their arms flying in the air. As Alexis turned back to the front he heard the sounds of shots being fired. Several more reports from rifles sounded around the two as they ran. Within a minute they reached the edge of the woods and continued running in the direction of Frenchtown.[31]

Escape to Frenchtown
by Lynn Reaume

Escape to Frenchtown
January 19, 1813

The sun rose over Frenchtown and revealed the bodies and bloodshed from the previous day's battle. Darkness had kept the Kentucky soldiers from tending to the dead in the woods the night before, so a detail was sent out by Lt. Colonel Lewis early in the morning to retrieve the bodies. A group of 100 men were sent out. Twelve bodies were found; all but one stripped and scalped in the night by the Indians. While the soldiers were busy with their detail, Colonel Lewis sent an express message to General Winchester at the Maumee River Rapids encouraging the General to send reinforcements to the Raisin.

The citizen soldiers of Frenchtown began to return to their homes in the early morning hours of January 19, 1813. Captain Ambrose Charland had disbanded his men after Colonel Lewis declined their offer to assist the army further. Lewis instead told Charland to dispatch his men back to their homes to protect their families in case the Indians returned. The habitants also offered to turn over to the American army all the supplies, which the British had been collecting for themselves.

Etienne LeBeau was hesitant to leave the settlement after the fight. He was confident that his father, René, was secure at the family cabin at Sandy Creek. Instead, Etienne went to the house of Jean-Baptiste Couture along with several Kentucky officers who sought shelter from the cold.

The morning sun filtered through the thin panes of glass that remained in the Couture cabin. Many of the windows had been broken out during the battle the night before. Jean-Baptiste had stubbornly returned to his *homestead* after the fighting, and insisted on staying despite protests from Colonel Lewis. He had conceded instead to house as many of the soldiers that he could through the night.

Morning brought new discoveries of the battle. Many of the residents of Frenchtown had suffered damage to their homes. The men who remained in the settlement set off shortly after dawn to help their neighbors any way they could. The soldiers who did not go on detail gathering bodies, remained to reinforce the *pickets* which surrounded the settlement proper.

Etienne joined Jean-Baptiste Couture as he gathered materials to help reconstruct some of the more severely damaged homes. The soldiers who lodged with him were long gone tending to orders from their commanding officers. Etienne shouldered an axe and set off in the direction of Jean-Baptiste Jerome's house where the Kentucky soldiers were beginning to collect the bodies of the fallen. The door to the Jerome cabin stood open as Etienne approached. Several Kentucky soldiers were standing around the front of the house, talking, he guessed, about the detail from which they had returned.

"Those Indians sure made a mess out there," one soldier commented nodding his head in the general direction of the wooded area north of Frenchtown.

"It's just like an Indian to turn tail, then come back later and gather whatever he can get his hands on . . ." a second soldier added sharply.

Etienne passed the soldiers and continued through the settlement. His thoughts turned briefly to his family as he spied two young children covered in blankets just past the Jerome cabin. A crowd was growing around them. Cries could be heard over the commotion. Etienne listened to the laments as they rose in the air.

"They killed our Papa," Alexis sobbed. "It was those Indians. They did it."

Genevieve sat silent as her brother wailed out his outrage at the events of the night before. They had reached Frenchtown quickly through the woods driven by the need to get away from the Indians and by the cold stinging of their bare feet. As soon as the settlement was within sight, Alexis began calling out to all who could hear. He continued his shouts as men and women cautiously peered through windows and doorways at the sound. Alexis shouted and ran his way to the house of Jean-Baptiste Jerome. Genevieve, slowed her pace as the settlement came within sight. The events of the night left her physically and emotionally exhausted. Determined to hold back the tears, which threatened, Genevieve followed Alexis to the nearest house. When she reached his side she was grateful to see that Madame Jerome had remained at the settlement through the battle. Alexis and Genevieve were quickly covered with blankets and set upon a log near an open fire to warm themselves.

Etienne could not believe his ears. The sound from the lad was too familiar. Pushing his way between the onlookers, Etienne froze in his tracks as the faces of his young brother and sister came into view. Alexis stopped his accusations and cried at the sight of his older brother. "Etienne!"

The sound of her brother's voice brought Genevieve out of her shock. She raised her head and met the steady glare of Etienne, now moving closer to the two young LeBeaus. Etienne reached her side as she was standing, throwing the blanket to the ground in her haste. She threw her arms around Etienne and her sobs returned in full force. Etienne placed his hand at the back of Genevieve's head and comforted her sudden flow of tears. Her body jerked suddenly as she let a cry escape her lips. Alexis leaped to his feet and grabbed his brother around the legs. The three of them stood together as the crowd of people grew silent.

Etienne gently nudged Genevieve away from his chest and looked into her face. Her tear-streaked cheeks were red from cold. Her eyes shone with sadness that Etienne had yet to understand.

"Papa . . ." was all Genevieve could say as she trembled from the cold.

"Hush, now. I am here, Vieve." Etienne soothed.

"Etienne," a small voice from his calves began. Etienne looked down at Alexis and motioned for him to stand. Several minutes passed before Etienne felt he could speak. Someone gathered the blanket Genevieve had been wearing and wrapped it about her shoulders once more. "Vieve, why are you here? What happened?" Etienne asked swallowing the knot that had formed in his throat.

Genevieve took several deep breaths and stepped back out of her brother's protective arms. "Last night . . . after dark . . ." She told Etienne the details of the horrors that occurred at Sandy Creek.

Cross of St. Antoine
by Lynn Reaume

St. Antoine's

So much sadness surrounded the LeBeau children as they stood together at St. Antoine's Church. No tears flowed today. Everyone was too weary from crying in the days before the burial. Eight–year-old Alexis had been too young when his mother died to remember anything about what happened. However, the images he would see on that snow-covered morning of January 21 would be burned into his memory forever.

Wartime shortages made it difficult, but enough walnut boards had been found to make two sizeable coffins, broad at the shoulders and tapering to a narrow width at the foot. The bodies were wrapped tightly in linen and placed inside. They were buried in shallow graves dug behind St. Antoine's Church.

Alexis Loranger[32] was in charge of conducting and recording burials in the absence of a resident priest. Little Alexis had always smiled whenever they met, perhaps because they shared the same first name. There were no smiles that day however.

No mass could be said. Only a priest could do that. But as *Church Cantor*, Alexis Loranger said some comforting words, then prayed and chanted a beautiful hymn in Latin. Although he couldn't understand the words, little Alexis felt somehow better after hearing Loranger's musical voice. Genevieve later explained that now their father had gone to join their mother in a far better place, a place where they wouldn't have to worry about wars or anything else.

A tear streaked down Genevieve's cheek as the small procession left the gravesite. Margaret placed a gentle hand on Genevieve's back and offered some comforting words. With a nod Genevieve paused to look back at the newly broken ground where her father lay. She took a deep breath and followed her brothers and sister to a waiting sleigh that would return them to the safety of the Navarre house.

Etienne carefully steered his father's sleigh along the path back toward Frenchtown. As he drove, his thoughts wandered back to the day he found Alexis and Genevieve trembling in the snow. He had taken the children to the house of Lt. Colonel Francis Navarre where Margaret LeBeau Couture was staying. Once he was assured the children would be cared for, he set out to find Colonel Lewis. Instead, he found Captain Charland and informed him of the incident the night before at Sandy Creek. Charland sent word to Lewis and waited for a reply as Etienne paced impatiently through the snow. When word came, Charland informed Etienne that Colonel Lewis did not intend to send a detachment to Sandy Creek.

"Ambrose," Etienne protested. "My father is lying in his house. We must retrieve the bodies for a proper burial. Won't you help me?"

Charland felt the anger in Etienne and understood the pain the young man felt. He quickly gathered a small force of residents to go to Sandy Creek. It was guided by Joseph Navarre, an experienced woodsman. The leader, however, was the 58-year-old cousin of Baptiste Soleau, a shadowy character named Jean-Baptiste Sanscrainte.[33] Fearless John, as he was called, was good at playing one side against the other. He held two paying jobs; both as an Indian agent for the Americans and , at the same time, as Indian interpreter for the British. Surely, if anyone could get them through, it would be him.

Of course, Etienne went along. So did Alexis Sanscrainte, Joseph Menard, Medard Labadie, Joseph

LaTour, and three of the Nadeau brothers.[34]   Alexis
Loranger, the *Church Cantor*, went along as well. They
encountered a small group of Indians as they approached
the LeBeau house, but after a brief exchange of gunfire,
they were able to recover the bodies of both René LeBeau
and Baptiste Soleau.

WINCHESTER'S HEAD-QUARTERS.

House of Francois Navarre
from Lossing's "Field Book of the War of 1812"

61

Home of Francis Navarre
Evening of January 21, 1813

The Navarre house was extremely busy. *"Bonjour mes enfants,"* Madame Navarre[35] greeted the three mourners as they entered the door. Genevieve's eyes remained downcast as she returned their cousin's greeting. She quietly excused herself from the parlor and went to the girls' sleeping quarters as far away as possible from the noise and confusion.

Margaret sighed as Genevieve left the room. Gathering her emotions, she turned to young Alexis and smiled. "You okay, Lexi?"

"Of course, Meg," he answered. "Who wouldn't be with all these soldiers around? Did you see all those men who rode with General Winchester?[36] I sure would like to get in that room where he set up his *headquarters*."

Margaret smiled again. "I'm glad to see you're feeling better. Go and see if Robert Navarre is in the barn. He may need help with the General's horses."

Alexis ran out the door toward the barn. He could see several men coming and going from the Navarre house. The barn stood tall and sturdy in the winter wind. The past few days, several inches of snow had fallen on Frenchtown, leaving large mounds piled against each building.

"Close that door," Robert Navarre scolded as Alexis entered. He shook the snow from his shoes and walked softly to the side of the oldest Navarre child.

"My sister told me to help you with the horses," Alexis challenged.

"You think you are up to it?" Robert teased. "Start over there. We need to brush their coats. Here on the wall, use this brush." Robert handed Alexis a brush and went back to his work.

Alexis reached for the saddle of the nearest horse. He began to unbuckle the leather as Robert looked up.

"No Alexis," Robert began. "That is my father's best horse. He wants to leave it for General Winchester in case something happens tonight."

"What could happen?" Alexis asked warily.

"Messengers have been in and out of here constantly. Colonel Wells wants to realign the army. Winchester doesn't. Wells left with Captain Langham to meet Harrison's army. The regulars are not too happy being left without much of a *breastworks* to defend them." Robert continued.

Alexis nodded and moved on to the next horse. After everything that had happened, he wasn't happy at the thought of another battle. Forgetting what he was doing, he dropped the horse brush and ran out the barn door. He wanted to see Genevieve. She would tell him that they would be safe. He had been brave, but now, again, he was scared.

That evening, Alexis lay on the upstairs floor of the Navarre house, his eyes wide open. He knew he should have fallen asleep hours before, but his mind still raced with thoughts of the funeral and the events of the previous few days. Now, with what Robert had said about there being more Americans coming, there was sure to be more trouble. Alexis wished Etienne had stayed with them, but at least Genevieve was there.

Others were obviously not having trouble sleeping. He could hear the heavy snoring of General Winchester coming from the room below. Alexis shifted positions trying to get more comfortable. "No doubt," he thought to himself, "after their nightcap of wine and brandy, the General and his staff are sleeping quite contentedly next to the great fireplace. It's kind of odd that they're in the same room where Indians stay when visiting the Navarres."

Suddenly he heard the loud voice of Colonel Navarre calling from downstairs. Then came the noise of pounding footsteps as Navarre sent his son, Robert, into the room to awaken General Winchester.

Alexis could hear Robert yelling, "General! General! Wake up! Your army is being attacked!"

Soon everyone was up and running in confusion. Alexis called for his sister as he tried to avoid being trampled in the darkness. The crowd of military staff and family members tried to part as Winchester stumbled towards the door, but everyone was packed too closely together. Unable to force his way through to the front door, Winchester turned towards the window and opened the shutters wide.

He climbed through the window frame just as Navarre's already saddled horse was brought up to the house. Mounting from the windowsill, he rode off at a gallop, leaving his overcoat behind. He was followed by his staff officers, as soon as they managed to dress and get their horses. As the confusion died down, the sounds of gunfire could be heard clearly in the distance. Alexis lay curled in a ball with his blanket tucked tightly around him.

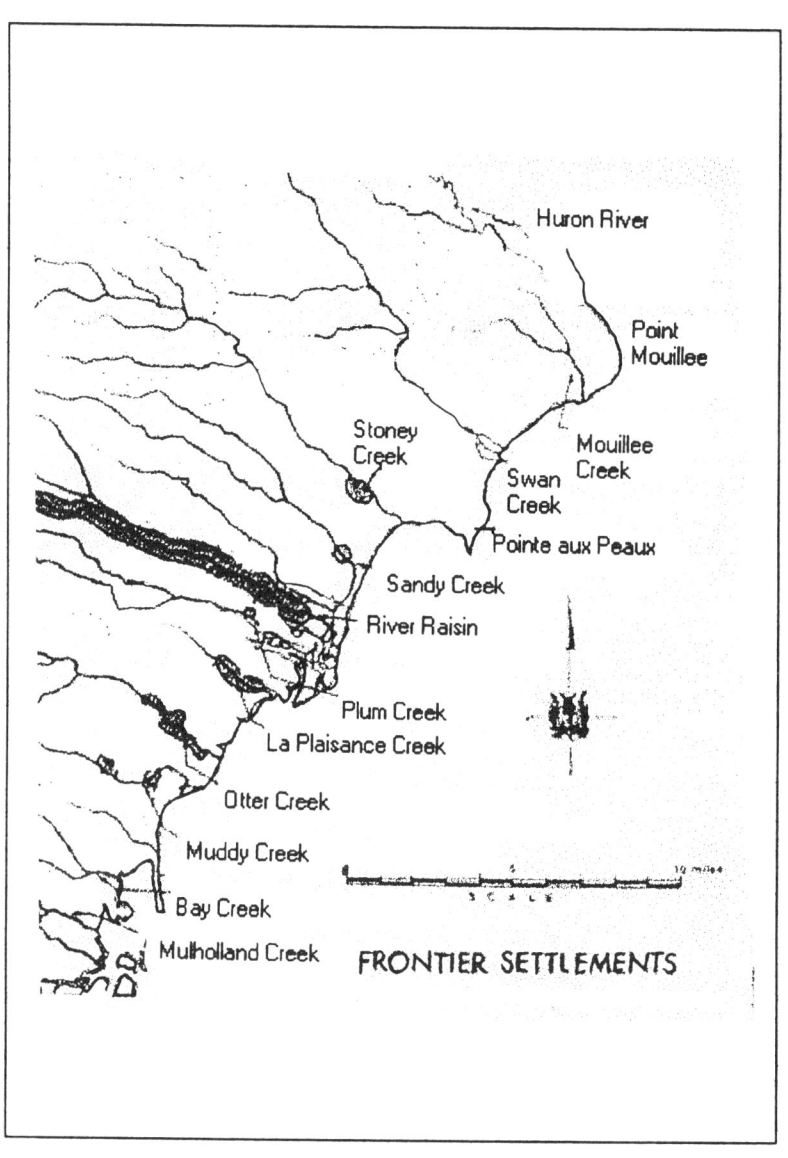

Map of Settlements Along Michigan's Lake Erie Shoreline
from "Legacy of the River Raisin"

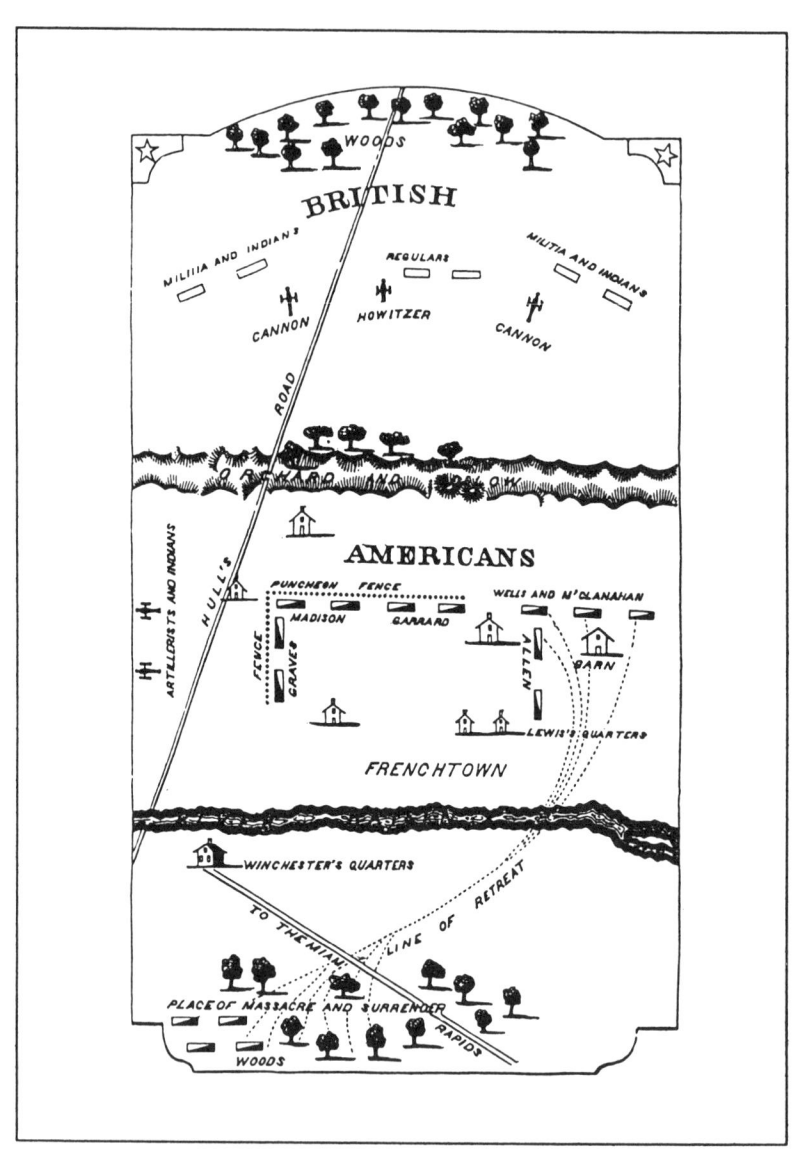

British Battle Map
from Bulkley's "History of Monroe County"

Battle of the River Raisin
January 22, 1813

Etienne LeBeau began to wipe the sleep from his eyes. He had just spent another uncomfortable night sleeping on the floor at Jean-Baptiste Couture's house. There was a bed in the room, but it was full of American officers. Three of them were sleeping crossways on it, with their feet hanging over the edge of the mattress.

The women and children had already been sent to the Navarre house, 3/4 of a mile upriver, but the men had stayed to protect their property. Suddenly, he could feel someone tugging at his arm. It was Jean-Baptiste's son, Medard, who said,

"Come on *mon ami,* let's get going. I know something is about to happen. I just know it. We better go out and have a look around."

Rubbing his eyes with his free hand, Etienne allowed himself to be pulled to his feet. Already dressed, he threw on his capote and followed Medard outside. On the way out, Medard stopped and gave the American drummer boy a gentle kick. The young man groaned, and then, still wrapped in his gray woolen blanket, slipped on his *moccasins,* picked up his drum, and followed the others out the door.

The camp was already stirring as the drummer began to beat a tune called *"Three Camps"* as a signal for those still asleep to get up. Suddenly, the relative quiet was interrupted by a shot in the direction of the northern fence line. This was followed by others, then the early morning darkness was brightened by the flashing trail of a howitzer shell. As they watched, the first shell flew high over their heads and struck the Robert house across the river. It was only then that Etienne realized they were under a full-scale British attack.

Medard ran back inside to get his father, but Etienne followed the nearby soldiers who were streaming out of the buildings and taking up defensive positions along the outer fences. From this point, Etienne was able to see much of the battle unfold.

Looking back over his shoulder, Etienne could make out the figures of Jean-Baptiste and Medard Couture. They were firing at the enemy from the upstairs windows of their cabin.

A few hundred yards downriver towards the Reaume farm, he saw the regular infantry formed up in front of the camp they had made outside the protection of Frenchtown's garden fences. For half an hour, they stood up against musket and cannon fire, but all the time, Indians were circling around behind them.

Then, on the opposite bank of the river, General Winchester appeared, riding Francois Navarre's best horse. Etienne watched, as he ordered the regulars to fall back to the protection of the riverbank. In all the confusion, however, the maneuver failed, and the regulars ran right across the slippery river ice, chased by the Indians.

Colonels Lewis and Allen went out to join Winchester, and several *companies* of Kentucky militia were sent out to rescue the fleeing regulars, but none came back. Etienne could hear gunfire as the troops disappeared across the river, but the sound was soon drowned out by more firing along the fences on all sides of the village.

Three times, the British and their Canadian allies tried to break through the fence lines. The British regulars looked frightening, drawn up in massive lines with shining bayonets fixed to the barrels of their muskets. But each time they advanced, the Kentucky militia drove them back with heavy casualties.

In between assaults, the enemy regrouped and found positions from which to snipe at the Kentuckians. They pushed their cannons closer and closer to the fence line. In addition, some Indians managed to sneak down along the riverbank and were firing through gaps in the fencing and between the houses.

But the Americans did not give up. The British *artillery* crews were so close, they made easy targets for the Kentucky *sharpshooters*. Individual volunteers rushed out from behind the fences to burn outlying farm buildings before the British occupied them.

The battle raged for almost 5 hours. But about 11 am, the firing finally stopped, and men bearing flags of truce were seen passing between the lines. Etienne had just about run out of powder and ball. He was also getting very hungry, so he decided to head back to Couture's house. Perhaps he could find more ammunition and some food.

As he approached, he could see Dr. Todd[37] taking the American Captain Hart[38] into the hospital, which had been set up in Jerome's house. The captain had been hit in the ankle by a shot that had passed through a gap in the fences. Nearby, a drum lay in the snow, and Etienne wondered what had become of the drummer.[39]

He also wondered where the Coutures had gone. He wondered, that is, until he saw Medard struggling through the snow. Stretched over Medard's back was the lifeless body of his father, Jean-Baptiste.

As Etienne rushed to help, Medard cried out, "It's no use! Papa is dead. We went outside the pickets with Captain Price's men to pick up the wounded Kentuckians who had been left behind when the right wing retreated across the river. But we fell into an ambush, ourselves. Captain Price and his men were cut to pieces. Quick, help me hide his body in our straw pile."

Etienne shot back a questioning glance, but Medard went on to explain, "We're surrounded and almost out of ammunition. General Winchester has been captured, and Major Madison has decided to surrender what's left of the American army. The British commander, Colonel Procter, has promised to protect our wounded from the vengeance of the Indians, but he cannot protect the dead. The Indians have threatened to kill anyone who gives their enemy a decent burial. If we can hide my father's body, I can come back tonight and bury him."

"Shouldn't we try to escape?" asked Etienne.

"You can if you want," came the reply. "but, I'm not leaving my father dead in his own yard. This is my home. Maybe, if I stay here, I can help the American doctors tend their wounded. "

"I...I...can't stay." stammered Etienne. "I've got to get back to take care of my little brother and sister at Navarre's house. Once the Kentuckians march out to surrender, the Indians will be all over us."

"Yes, I know. Don't worry about me. When you get to Navarre's, tell my mother what has happened. Tell her not to try to come back here. She shouldn't wait for me, but go to Detroit right away. After this, no one will be safe here anymore."[40]

The Departure
by Joe Lee

Flight from Frenchtown
January 22-23, 1813

Although the Navarre house was crowded with family and friends, there was very little noise. Voices were hushed as everyone listened to the sound of the gunfire downriver as it began to diminish. Even the children listened anxiously for any news on the outcome of the battle.

Out in the yard, Robert Navarre and his cousin "Platte" Navarre[41] were preparing some sleds in case they would be needed for a quick getaway. In fact, the last thing Robert's father, Colonel Navarre, had said to him before following after General Winchester that morning, was to get the rest of the family together and take them to the comparative safety of Detroit.

Back inside, little Alexis LeBeau was sitting at the table, his chin cupped in his hands. He couldn't believe it was happening all over again. Here they were, waiting for brother Etienne's return, just like they were 3 nights ago, when his father and uncle had been killed.

The waiting seemed like it would never end, but all of a sudden there was a shout: "Indians! The Indians are coming!"

Alexis flew into his sister's arms and hid his face in her *petticoat*. "Vieve, Vieve, don't let them hurt us!" he cried.

"Sush, Lexi. Be quiet," said Genevieve as she wrapped her arms around her trembling brother. "If they come inside, we must not let them see how frightened we are."

There was barely time for the children to compose themselves before the Indians threw open the unbarred door and rushed inside. Fierce as lions, the painted warriors swarmed all over the house, taking what they wanted and frightening the inhabitants completely.

Madame Couture was huddled with her children in a corner of the room, when she spied one tall Ottawa warrior wearing a bloody coat. "That's my husband's coat," she gasped, "That belongs to Jean-Baptiste!" She broke down in tears as she realized that her husband was no more.

The Indians took no heed, however, and set to searching the house. Once they were satisfied that the inhabitants were not hiding any escaped Kentuckians, they left, taking only a few small items they could easily carry.

As the tall Ottawa reached the door, however, he stopped and stared intently at young Genevieve. She clutched Alexis to her as tightly as she could, to the point were he had to struggle to breath. But the towering warrior half smiled and said, "You see, we are not *savages*. We don't make war on defenseless widows and orphans." Then, in a flash, he was out the door. Genevieve breathed a sigh of relief, and released her gasping brother.

Robert and Platte came in soon after the Ottawas had left. "They didn't bother us at all," exclaimed Robert, "Once we explained we were taking our families to Detroit, they let us keep our ponies. But, one tall fellow told us we better hurry up. Some of the other Indians are in a bad mood and Tecumseh is not here to control them. They want to kill the wounded Kentuckians who were taken prisoner, and they might hurt us, too."

"But what about Etienne?" cried Genevieve. "Alexis and I have to wait for our brother. I know he will come for us."

These words were no sooner uttered than a chorus of similar objections rose from the other people in the house. All were worried about their relatives and friends who had been caught up in the battle. None wanted to abandon them until they had learned of their fate.

So the group remained through the night of the 22nd of January, but in the early morning hours on the 23rd, an Indian brought word from Francois Navarre that he was now a prisoner and was being sent to Fort Malden. The settlement was to be left unprotected, and the local population was ordered to leave. Navarre's instructions were for Robert to take the family to Detroit immediately, without waiting for anyone.

By the time Robert's *traineau* was loaded with his mother and 11 brothers and sisters, there wasn't much room left for Alexis and Genevieve. But Robert managed to squeeze them both on, with Alexis sitting on his sister's lap. This left no room for Robert, so he braced himself on the front of the sled, with his feet resting on the *thills*. Several families from the River Raisin gathered at the Navarre's on their way to safety. As the little convoy of sleds headed out, the skies were turning a dark gray, and it was starting to sleet.

On their way north, they were joined by other sled trains, all filled with refugees heading away from the carnage and desolation which they had once called home. The trip would take the rest of the day and all through the night. Before dawn, all would be soaked and chilled to the bone as the sleet turned to rain.

Driving one of the sleds was a feisty 80-year-old woman named Rachel Knaggs. She was one of the few "Yankee" settlers who had remained in the settlement after its surrender the previous summer. Her sons hated the British and one, Whitmore Knaggs, was captured during the battle on the 22nd. She, herself, was caught trying to hide one of the American soldiers in an old, empty barrel in her house. One of the Indians took her coat, and several others dragged her off to Colonel Procter, who ordered her out of town.

Genevieve saw that Mrs. Knaggs had no coat to keep her warm, so she held up a blanket. Instead of accepting the offer, the old woman cracked a whip over her pony's head. As she sped past, she yelled, "You keep your blanket, girlie, my spunk will keep me warm!"

Somehow, after that, Genevieve knew they were going to make it. Her only worry was for Etienne.

Heading for Detroit
by Joe Lee

Safety in Detroit
January 24, 1813

As Etienne traveled the road to Detroit, his thoughts wandered back to his family. The last he saw of them, they were safely within the walls of the Navarre house, but when he had arrived there late on the day after the battle, the home stood empty. He could only hope they had made it safely to Detroit ahead of him.

On his journey to Detroit he had encountered few people. Now, as he approached the city, Etienne could see a couple of pony sleds racing toward him down the slush-covered road. He raised a hand to his eyes to shield them from the sun that was rising on the horizon in order to get a better look. As the sleds came closer, Etienne recognized the two drivers. They were Robert Navarre and Platte Navarre. Etienne waved his arms to get the attention of the drivers. Robert Navarre spotted him and slowed his pony.

"Etienne! We were afraid you were dead," Robert exclaimed in surprise. He pulled the reins of the sled and stopped a few yards past Etienne.

"Robert, where is my family? I went to your father's house after I escaped, but everyone was gone." Etienne asked.

"Late afternoon we started for Detroit. You should have seen these sleds packed with people." Robert answered.

"So Genevieve and Alexis are in Detroit then? Where can I find them?"

"I took my mother and brother and sisters to our grandparents' farm. Madame Couture and her family, as well as your sisters and brother were still there when I left this morning. I have been ordered to go back to Frenchtown to help the British carry wounded back to Fort

Malden." With a crack of the whip, Robert and Platte began their journey down the road that Etienne had just traveled.

Upon reaching the settlement, Etienne began to feel weary. He had on several occasions traveled to the Navarre farm when he was in Detroit for trading. He walked on tired legs until he saw the house in the distance. Overcome with fatigue, Etienne fell to his knees in the mud and snow.

From the window Alexis spied a figure approach. The man stopped, looked toward the house and fell to his knees. "Vieve, there is someone outside. Do you think he is hurt?"

Genevieve walked to the window where Alexis was perched. She looked out the window and immediately recognized the figure in the snow. "Alexis, don't you see? It is Etienne!"

Alexis, in his excitement, threw open the casement windows and bounded out into the snow shrieking, "Etienne! Etienne! I knew you would come!" Then turning toward the house he called excitedly, "Vieve, it is Etienne!"

At the sound of his brother's voice, Etienne rose to his feet. Before Etienne could take a step, Alexis jumped up into his arms. Genevieve closely followed Alexis' footsteps. He reached Etienne as he placed Alexis back on the ground. "You are really here?" she ventured.

"Yes, Vieve. We've made it to safety, all of us . . . our family."

"What will we do now?" Alexis asked.
Etienne took his younger brother by the hand and smiled. "For now we will stay in Detroit. It should be safe here for some time."

"What if the war continues for years?" Genevieve cautiously asked.

"The war can't go on forever. We have each other. We will survive, and someday . . ." Etienne's reply hung unfinished.

"Someday what?" Alexis asked curiously.

Taking his brother and sister into his arms Etienne replied, "Someday we will go home. *Nous irons chez nous.*"

A Refugee Returns
by Joe Lee

Aftermath

The destruction of Frenchtown commenced the day after the battle when vengeful Indians burned down the homes of Jean-Baptiste Jerome and Hubert LaCroix, which were being used as hospitals for the Kentucky soldiers who had been wounded in the battle.

Over the next few months, many of the farms along the River Raisin and Sandy Creek would share the same fate. The family of Jean-Baptiste Couture, lost all their hogs, four cows, 30 sheep, their house, barn, stable, bake house, a great quantity of wheat, corn, oats, hay and all their personal possessions.

Many habitants fled to Detroit or other nearby towns. The more fortunate, like Rachel Knaggs[42], found relatives or friends to stay with. Her daughter Elizabeth, the wife of Colonel John Anderson[43], even had enough money to ransom some of the Kentuckians who had been taken prisoner by the Indians. The less fortunate settlers, however, like the Charlands, were reduced to begging on the street. Some, such as Hubert LaCroix, were arrested as American sympathizers and imprisoned by the British.

A little less than half the population chose to remain at the River Raisin. They were mostly French habitants who were banking on their formerly friendly relations with the Potawatomies to protect them from harm. In fact, some of the Indians urged these settlers to join the British side, but there were no volunteers, not after all that had happened.[44]

Colonel Procter, who had led the British forces from Fort Malden to victory at the River Raisin, considered the remaining habitants to be a nest of traitors and violators of their parole, especially after some of the younger settlers chose to join the American forces under General Harrison at Fort Meigs. He wanted to destroy what remained of their settlement, but Chief Tecumseh would not hear of it. "The day the River Raisin is destroyed," he warned, "Malden will burn."

Procter needn't have worried. Although Francis Navarre and others led an underground resistance movement against the British, most of the habitants had more than enough to do just to stay alive. By the time John Anderson returned with a new American army to liberate Frenchtown in the fall of 1813, the people had nothing left to eat except muskmelons and fruit. To get themselves through the following winter, they ate boiled and salted hay and roasted muskrats.[45]

Despite the hardships and the continuation of the war, many habitants tried to return to rebuild their homes during 1813 and 1814. Francois Gandon returned to find even his fruit trees had been destroyed. Charred skeletons littered the ruins of his burned-out farmhouse.

What was left of the LeBeau family would not return until after the Treaty of Ghent[46] was signed on Christmas Eve of 1814. Even with the end of the war, life remained hard along the River Raisin. So much had been destroyed that John Anderson went to Washington, D. C., to plead for help from the government.

It would take many years to rebuild the settlement. In 1817, Governor Cass[47] reorganized the River Raisin country and named it Monroe County in honor of James Monroe,[48] the new President of the United States. Yankee settlers from New York and other eastern states began to pour into the area, especially after the Erie Canal was opened in 1825. Although the old habitants would have quite a difficult time adjusting to the changes, future peace and prosperity for their old settlement was now assured.

Biographies

Alexis LeBeau:

Alexis was born June 4, 1804, at Sandy Creek, and baptized July 24 of the same year at Assumption Church in Sandwich, Ontario.

After the events which destroyed his home at Sandy Creek, Alexis lived in Detroit for two years with his brother, Etienne. In 1815, they returned to Sandy Creek.

Alexis married Angelica Lenfant in 1825 at St. Antoine's Church on the River Raisin. Together, they had 18 children, the fifth being born on January 20, 1833. This son was named January René LeBeau. He was born two days after the twentieth anniversary of Alexis' father's death.

Alexis was married three times, but had no additional children with his second or third wives. He died at the age of 82, and his funeral was held at St. Mary's Church in Monroe, Michigan, on July 19, 1886.

Genevieve LeBeau:

Genevieve was born June 21, 1798, in St. Antoine's Parish. After the War of 1812, she remained in Detroit. On February 22, 1814, she married Jean-Baptiste Savignac. She was fifteen years old. Together she and Jean-Baptiste had eight children. Her first husband died in August of 1834. She then married Joseph Parisien on August 11, 1835, and had three children. Joseph was buried on January 26, 1849. Genevieve was buried in Detroit on July 18, 1851.

Etienne LeBeau:

Etienne was born August 2, 1792, at Detroit. After joining Alexis and Genevieve in Detroit, Etienne married Mary Judith Chauvin on September 20, 1815. They had six children, three boys and three girls.

Mary Joseph LeBeau Soleau:

Mary Joseph was born on September 3, 1790, in Detroit. She married Jean-Baptiste Soleau at St. Antoine's, January 26, 1807. She gave birth to their third child on February 4, 1813, 17 days after the death of her husband at Sandy Creek. This son, William, was buried five days later.

On September 20, 1814 she married James Borgeat dit Provencal and had seven children by the time of his death in 1832.

She married a third time to Joseph Knapp on April 29, 1835. This union produced no children. However, he had four from a previous marriage.

Marie-Joseph passed away at the age of 67 and was buried at St. Anne's in Detroit on November 16, 1857.

Margaret LeBeau Couture:

Margaret was born January 20, 1796, in Detroit. She married Etienne Couture at St. Antoine's on April 21, 1811. They had three children, Etienne, Margaret, and Monica. Margaret died, at the age of 26, during childbirth of her fourth child. Both were buried March 6, 1822 at St. Antoine's. Her husband remarried in 1825 and had four more children.

Robert Navarre:

The oldest son of Colonel Francis Navarre, Robert was considered the first white male to be born at the River Raisin settlement. He was born on September 11, 1791. During the War of 1812, Robert played a significant role in helping his family to safety after the second Battle of the River Raisin. After the War, Robert made Frenchtown his home and continued to live within the area of Monroe with his wife Monica Duchene, whom he married on June 5, 1823. He and his wife had ten children.

In 1872, Robert attended a reunion of veterans of the War of 1812. George Armstrong Custer was the master of ceremonies. The average age of the men at the reunion was 90.

Robert was the last living survivor in Monroe from the original settlement at Frenchtown. He was buried at St. Joseph's Cemetery on December 21, 1881.

Tecumseh:

After the Battle of the River Raisin, the Shawnee leader continued to aid the British army with his confederation of warriors. However, the Battle of Lake Erie enabled the Americans to rid the country of the British army. Cut off from supplies, the British retreated back to Canada. Tecumseh's warriors followed the retreating army as they continued through Upper Canada toward the Thames River. On October 5, 1813, Tecumseh persuaded General Procter to stand and fight the Americans. This resulted in the Battle of the Thames. The Americans defeated the British army, and Tecumseh was killed while leading his warriors. His body was never recovered.

Colonel Procter:

After the Battle of the Thames, Procter, now a General, was brought up on charges of deserting his army. The British government held a court martial, but Procter was found not guilty. This did, however, end his active duty. He retired to England where he lived to be 59 years old. He died on Halloween, October 31, 1822, leaving a widow with four children.

17th U.S. Regiment:

Raised in Kentucky, this American unit was nearly destroyed by the Battles of the River Raisin. The few men who got away to Fort Meigs joined the 19th Infantry and the Kentucky Mounted Riflemen.

These men went on to face the British 41st Regiment of Foot several more times during the war of 1812, including the Battles at Mackinaw, Fort Stephenson, Fort Meigs, and the Battle of the Thames.

Glossary

American Long Knives: What the Native American warriors called the American soldiers.

Anishinabemowin: *(ah nish nah bay moh win)* The Indian (Potawatomi or Ojibwa) language.[49]

Artillery: People or objects related to the use of cannons.

Au secours!:   *(oh s'koor)* Help!

Bonjour: *(bohn JOO)* A French greeting meaning "good day" or "hello".

Bonjour mes enfants: *(bohn joo may zawn FAWN)* A French phrase meaning "hello my children."

Breastworks: Materials built up to protect soldiers from enemy fire.

Buckshot: Small caliber projectiles used originally for shooting at deer.

Capote: *(kah POHT)* A long, wool garment sometimes referred to as a blanket coat, usually equipped with a hood and tied around the waist with a sash.

Charette: *(shah RETT)* A French pony cart.

Chemise: *(shuh MEEZ)* A gown worn by women, girls and young boys as underwear, night shirts, and blouses.

Church Cantor: Choir director.

D'où viens-tu bergère?:   *(doo vyan TIEW, bayr JAYRuh)* Where do you come from Shepherdess?

Embers: The glowing red of a fire when most of the wood has been burned.

Habitants: *(ah bee TAWHN)* The first settlers at the River Raisin.

Headquarters: A place of command for the officers of an army.

Huzzah: A cry of exclamation like "Hooray."

Gristmill: Mill that takes grain and grinds it into flour.

Nous irons chez nous: *(new zee rohn shay new)* We will go home.

Moccasins: Deerskin shoes worn by Indians, Frenchmen, and the Kentucky soldiers at the River Raisin.

Mon ami: *(moh nah MEE)* My friend.

Mon fils: *(mohn FEESS)* My son.

Mon petit: *(mohn p'TEE)* My little one (kid).

Mon vieux: (*mohn VIEW*) My old man! Old buddy.

M'sieur: (*m'SIEW*) Mister or Mr.

Muskets: Weapons used by British and American soldiers during the War of 1812 (guns).

Musket balls: The ammunition or bullets used in a musket.

Oui: (*WEE*) yes.

Petticoat: The outer skirt worn by women and girls in the late 17th century and early 18th century.

Pickets: The fence that surrounded the homes at Frenchtown.

Priming pan: A part of the musket lock holding the priming charge of gunpowder which is used to set off the main charge within the musket barrel.

Que'est-ce qui est arrivé?: (*kess kee eh tah ree VAY*) What happened?

Redware: A type of coarse, low-fired, inexpensive ceramic or pottery, colored red, often used on the frontier.

S'il te plaît: (*seel tuh PLAY*) Please (if it pleases you.)

Savages: A common white settler's way of referring to the Native American warriors.

Scalping: The act of cutting off the top of someone's hair and head.

Sharpshooters: Kentucky riflemen and Native American warriors who excelled at shooting from behind trees and fences, or other types of hiding places.

Saint Antoine à la Rivière aux Raisins:
(san awn TWAHN ah lah ree vyair oh ray ZAN) The Catholic church at Frenchtown, about 4 miles west of the settlement.

Thills: The shafts of a vehicle that attach the horse to it.

Tourtières: *(tohr TYAIR)* Meat pies.

Traineau: *(tray NOH)* Sled.

Volleys: The firing of a group muskets all at the same time to increase the shock effect of firepower during battle.

Voyage: Trip or voyage. A form of this French word was used to describe the canoe paddlers, or *voyageurs*, who worked in the fur trade.

Bibliography

In constructing this story, the authors referred as much as possible to original documents and family recollections. We also made frequent use of the published works listed below. The most complete, factual description of the battle may be found in Dennis Au's book, <u>War on the Raisin.</u> During his tenure as Assistant Director, Mr. Au assembled a lot of background material in the Museum Archives, which we found useful in our writing.

Antal, Sandy. <u>A Wampum Denied: Procter's War of 1812.</u>
    Canada: Carleton University Press, 1997.

Au, Dennis M. <u>War on the Raisin.</u> Flat Rock: Monroe
    County Historical Commission, 1981.

Austerberry, John. "Christmas on the River Raisin, 200
    years ago." <u>Monroe Evening News,</u> 24 Dec., 1984.

Bartolo, Ghislaine, and Lynn Reaume. <u>The Cross Leads
    Generations On.</u> New York: Custombook, 1988.

Bulkley, J. M. <u>History of Monroe County, Michigan</u>.
    Chicago: Lewis Publishing Company, 1913.

Clift, G. Glenn. <u>Remember the Raisin.</u> Frankfort:
    Kentucky Historical Society, 1961.

Coles, Harry L. <u>The War of 1812.</u> Chicago: University of
    Chicago Press, 1965.

Denissen, Rev. Christian. <u>French Families of the Detroit
    River Region 1701-1936.</u> Detroit: Detroit
    Genealogical Research, 1987.

Lossing, Benson J. <u>The Pictorial Field Book of the War of
    1812.</u> Reprint. New York: Benchmark Publishing
    Corp., 1970.

Rissover, Jean. <u>The French Colonial Christmas Book.</u>
    Missouri: St. Genevieve Press, 1991.

Wing, Talcott S. <u>History of Monroe County.</u> New York:
    Munsell and Co., 1890

The Eve of the Millennium

The bulk of this book was written in 1999, on the Eve of the Millennium. As people began to prepare for the celebration of the year 2000, a singular event occurred.

A century and a half earlier, the old Church and Cemetery of St. Antoine had been abandoned, and the land was eventually sold off as farmland. A small park was dedicated to mark the spot where the church building and cemetery had once been located.

In the summer of 1999, the remaining farmland was purchased for a housing development. Huge machines pushed tons of dirt around as storm sewers and a roadway were put in. In August, heavy rains began to wash away the disturbed soil, revealing a scattering of broken bones. The bones were taken to the Monroe County Health Department for analysis. They turned out to be human, the remains of at least two individuals.

Since this was the cemetery in which Rene LeBeau and Baptiste Soleau were buried, it is tempting to pretend that these bones may be theirs. If so, why have they appeared now, at the dawn of a new millennium?

Perhaps their message is very simple. As we stand, facing the next thousand years, they have come to remind us not to forget our past. Both our present and our future are built upon it. As residents of Monroe County, we all share a rich heritage and a unique place in history. We, the authors, hope this book will help others to appreciate that heritage.[50]

Notes

¹ This word has been spelled in various ways over the years. We used Frederic Baraga's <u>Dictionary of the Ojibway Language</u> to translate the words "river" and "sturgeon" and came up with the spelling used in the text. Other historical accounts name the river as the Namet Cybi, Nummassippi, or Numaseepee.

² The actual translation was the River of Grapes. It was often written in the singular (r. au raisin.) This is one of the few streams in Monroe County which never had its name translated completely into English.

³ In early documents, Navarre is listed as both Francis and Francois. Each seems to be used as often as the other.

⁴ This name has not been translated at present, but may relate to Francois' relationship with the Potawatomies, continuing in the footsteps of his father, Robische (Robert) who was often called "the Speaker." The closest I can come in Baraga's Ojibway dictionary is "Tchingwan," meaning "Meteor."

⁵ The story of how Navarre got his land can be found in the <u>History of Monroe County Michigan</u> by Talcott Wing.

⁶ This parish was first organized by Fr. Frechette of St Anne's Church in 1788. It was not until 1794, however, that the name was chosen in honor of St. Anthony, the patron saint of the poor. St Antoine's Church is generally considered the second oldest continuous parish in the state. In the mid 19ᵗʰ century the name was changed to St. Mary's Church in honor of the new order of the Sisters of the Immaculate Heart of Mary.

⁷ Also known as ribbon farms, these tracts of land were common to the Canadian French who primarily built along the banks of waterways. Each farm had a narrow frontage in order to give everyone access to water for drinking and transportation and to provide closeness to neighbors for mutual defense and social contact.

One local legend about the origin of ribbon farms states that the variable length of each farm was determined by the farmer and surveyor. They would set out from the front of the property with a jug of whisky. When the whisky ran out, the line was drawn to mark the end of the property.

[8] The idea of the children learning English from the priest is fictional, but not impossible. An Irishman, Fr. Edmund Burke, was assigned by the Bishop of Quebec as St. Antoine's first resident priest in 1794, but his conservative, pro-British stance made him unpopular with many of his parishioners. He left in 1796. Subsequent pastors were appointed by the Bishop of Baltimore. Fr. Levadoux periodically visited the parish from Detroit until the appointment of Fr. Dilhet in 1798. When Fr. Dilhet retired to Detroit in 1804, the parish was again dependent on visiting priests until 1822. Alexis Loranger, the resident choir director, had a hand in educating the locals, at least in religious matters.

[9] We have very few individual physical descriptions of our early settlers. Often a physical trait is only mentioned if it is unusual, such as Francois Gandon's blond hair. In the case of René LeBeau, family tradition mentioned he was 6'7" tall, a giant for his time.

[10] When General Hull reached the Maumee River, he found Luther Chapin's ship, the Cuyahoga (sometimes called the Cayauga or the Cuyahoga Packet) docked at the foot of the Rapids. Hull ordered the schooner and a smaller boat to be loaded with excess military supplies, personal luggage, and about 30 sick soldiers, and sent them to Detroit.
    It was only after their departure, as Hull's army was approaching the River Raisin, that word was received of the declaration of war. Hull sent ahead for Colonel Anderson to dispatch a boat to warn the Cuyahoga, but it was too late. Passing in range of the guns of British Fort Malden, the ship was boarded and captured. In the baggage, the British found papers describing Hull's forces and plans.

[11] Hull's army left the Rapids of the Maumee on July 1. Marching by way of old Fort Miamis, they made 12 miles that day, camping on a grassy plain about 18 miles from the River Raisin. On July 2, they arrived on the south bank of the Raisin, where they erected camp in a square, with their tents facing outward and their baggage in the center. Hull also held a grand review to impress the local citizens. The next day, they moved 9 miles north, to Swan Creek, where they spent the night, waiting for LaCroix's company of River Raisin militiamen to complete work on the bridge over the River Huron, about 6 miles

further north. On the 4th of July, they helped complete the bridge and passed the night taking turns, with half the men under arms while the other half slept. Their next camp would be at Springwells, well outside the River Raisin country.

[12] Hubert LaCroix, born in Montreal, was one of the earliest settlers along the Raisin. He was the first to answer the call for volunteers in 1812, and was unanimously elected captain of his company. Arrested by the British after Hull's surrender, he was released after Tecumseh interceded on his behalf. After the Battle of the River Raisin, however, he was again arrested and sent to Quebec. After the war was over, he rose to the rank of Colonel of Militia, was twice elected to the Legislative Council, and served as Sheriff of Monroe County. He died in 1827 at the age of 48. His mother's portrait, slit by a tomahawk during the war and preserved by his descendants, is currently on display at the River Raisin Battlefield Visitor Center in Monroe.

[13] There were two doctors in the Frenchtown settlement during this period. Dr. Peter Austin received an appointment as medical officer for the militia called into service and stationed at the River Raisin and along the Maumee. He was to be paid $33.33 per month, but was warned he would have to collect from the federal government, not the territorial authorities.

Dr. Joseph Dazette (Dazet), a native of France, was the first physician to establish himself on the River Raisin, arriving by the summer of 1804. He decided to purchase John Anderson's old trading post, which had been built in 1789 by Utreau Navarre. There he took care of the medical problems of most of the local French and Indian families. This is perhaps why his home, despite a few bullet holes, was never destroyed during the War of 1812. This building, now known as the Navarre-Anderson Trading Post, is the oldest standing log cabin in the state of Michigan, and is open to visitors in the summer.

[14] The battles of Brownstown and Monguagon are little known, yet they sealed the fate of Detroit in 1812. On August 5, Major Thomas Van Horne led 350 men south to break through the Indian blockade of Hull's supply road and escort a supply column back from Frenchtown on the River Raisin. Near Brownstown, they were ambushed and routed by Tecumseh and a relative handful of Indian warriors.

A second attempt to clear the road was more successful. With 600 troops, Lt. Colonel James Miller was able to defeat a combined force of British and Indians at Monguagon. He was aided in this by the spirited charge of DeQuindre's Detroit militia company, and by confusion between the British and their Indian allies who actually fired on each other at one point in the battle. However, the American army was too disorganized and exhausted to press their advantage and open the road all the way to the southern supply column, which was waiting under Captain Brush at the River Raisin.

Colonels Duncan McArthur and Lewis Cass were then sent with 300 men to make an end run around the Indian positions, but they failed to make their intended rendezvous with the River Raisin forces at Godfroy's trading post on the Huron River. By the time they returned, hungry and frustrated, to Detroit, General Hull had already made his decision to surrender.

[15] A number of River Raisin men, usually in small detachments, had taken part in the battles at Brownstown and Monguagon, and in the perilous duty of escorting the mail through the Indian lines to Detroit. Nonetheless, although some were wounded, we have no names of any specific individual Raisin militiamen who were killed.

The inhabitants of Frenchtown could not believe it when they first heard that General Hull had surrendered Detroit to the British. When Captain William Elliot of the First Essex Militia Regiment of Upper Canada arrived bearing papers announcing the surrender, Captain Brush had him locked up and denounced his papers as forgeries. Once the truth was established, however, Captain Brush and the Ohio militia fled the settlement, leaving Colonel Anderson and the local militia to conform to the terms of surrender.

The British seized any remaining public property and confiscated the settlers' firearms, leaving them completely at the mercy of the Indians. Many families fled the area, while others remained to endure pillaging and intimidation. Some known American sympathizers were arrested, but the bulk of the militia was placed on parole and allowed to return to their families, with the understanding they would not take up arms against the British again, unless properly exchanged for prisoners of war captured by the Americans.

[16] The high regard for Tecumseh is shown in a number of local family traditions. He gets Hubert LaCroix out of British captivity, forces the British to reimburse the Rivards for the loss of their oxen, and prevents further injury to Mrs. Anderson after a courageous standoff with the Indians in her parlor.

Some River Raisin militiamen told eyewitness stories about Tecumseh's death at the Battle of the Thames. Medard Labadie, James Knaggs, and Peter Navarre were said to have picked his body off the field and buried it to avoid desecration by vengeful American soldiers (although there is some doubt about Navarre even being at the battle.)

Genevieve LeBeau did not actually see the incident described here, but there is evidence from other sources that it did take place. Several Rulands owned property along the River Raisin. The Ruland family, of Dutch or German ancestry, had come from Long Island during the time of the American Revolution. Candidates for this incident include the families of Israel, Joseph, William, and Isaac Ruland. However, I believe our story involves the family of John Ruland (also known as Jean-Baptiste Roulin). His wife, Genevieve Toupin dit Dusseau, did not survive the war. She was buried in St-Antoine's Cemetery on Sept. 13, 1814. We have not been able to find names of their children.

[17] Local family traditions collected by Dennis Au indicate this was often used as a benediction for Christmas and the New Year.

[18]   "Bonjour, le maître et la maîtresse,
Et tout le monde du loger.
Si vous voulez nous rien donner, dites-le nous:
Nous vous demandons seulement la fille ainée!"
- from the diary of Eliz. Therese Baird of Mackinac Island

[19] Lt. Ambrose Charland had been in charge of the small stockade built at the Widow Robidoux's farm on Otter Creek when he received word to report for the surrender of Frenchtown on August 18, 1812. When Lewis' detachment from Winchester's army of Kentuckians arrived to liberate Frenchtown on January 18, 1813, he was one of the first settlers to arrive on the scene and apparently organized the local militia for the assault. During the battle on the 22nd, he was captured, but was released on parole. Upon his return home, he found that his wife, Angelique, had hidden one of the fleeing Kentuckians. The following day, after giving his only horse to the Kentuckian, Ambrose took his wife and 4-month-old baby and fled north to Detroit on foot across the ice. Having no family or friends in Detroit, the Charlands were forced to beg for food, and they suffered the loss of their baby. After the war, however, they returned to the River Raisin and raised 8 children.

[20] The Kentucky volunteers were mustered on August 15, 1812, at Georgetown Kentucky. This army was originally put together to reinforce the American garrison at Detroit. However, after Hull's surrender, their main objective became the liberation of Michigan Territory. From Georgetown, the troops crossed the Ohio River and continued a four-month march to the northern border of Ohio, at the Maumee Rapids. Along the way, these men endured hunger, exposure to the elements, and lack of supplies. By the time they reached the Rapids, the Kentuckians were tired and frustrated. Many of their enlistments were up, and this was their last chance to get at the enemy. After receiving appeals for help from American citizens at Frenchtown, General Winchester dispatched a force under Col. Lewis to liberate the settlement and seize the vital supplies the British were collecting there.

[21] The LaPlaisance Bay settlement was located south of the River Raisin, near LaPlaisance Bay, on Lake Erie. For many years before the mouth of the River Raisin was improved for shipping by the construction of the government canal, LaPlaisance Bay served as the main port for the Frenchtown settlement.

[22] Appointed to command the 2nd Michigan Militia Regiment by General Hull, John Anderson was the owner of a local trading post. Of Scottish ancestry, Anderson arrived at Frenchtown in this area from Montreal, where he had been ransomed as a boy from Indian captivity. His U.S. citizenship was confirmed in 1807.

In the summer of 1812, Anderson was forced to leave Frenchtown after death threats from the Indians. He left his wife, Elizabeth, and three children behind to care for the family's business. He was not present at Frenchtown during the battles of January, 1813, but returned with another American army in the Fall of that year. After the war, Anderson tried to relieve the suffering of the settlers and the Indians, finding homes for orphans and going to Washington to seek compensation for their losses. In Washington, he was arrested for trying to bribe a Congressman, but was released after explaining that was how he thought business was conducted there. Responsible for many civic and social improvements in Monroe, He died there in 1841, leaving behind two sons and a daughter.

[23] A long time Indian fighter, Bland Williams Ballard was 53 years old when he commanded the troops at Frenchtown. He was born in Virginia, and had come to Kentucky with his father in 1779. Indians in

Kentucky killed his father in 1788. After the war of 1812, Ballard became a major in the militia and died in 1853 at the age of 95.

[24] The son of the Reverend William Hickman, Paschal served in most of the Indian Wars in Kentucky from 1794 until he was appointed Captain in the 1st Rifle Regiment on June 8, 1812. Hickman was killed at the River Raisin on January 23, 1813. His mother died from grief over her son's death.

[25] William Lewis was born in Virginia, but became a resident of Jessamine County Kentucky. While serving in the U.S. army, he saw action against the Indians in the 1790's. On August 7, 1812, he received command of the 5th Kentucky Volunteer Militia Regiment, with the rank of Lt. Colonel. Lewis led his men through both battles at Frenchtown, but was captured during the disastrous retreat of the right wing. He was held as a prisoner of war in Quebec until 1814.

Benjamin Franklin Graves, born in Virginia, moved to Fayette County Kentucky in 1791. Until the War of 1812, he was a farmer and had been elected to the lower house of the Kentucky General Assembly. He was one of the wounded left at Frenchtown after the January 22nd battle, and was taken away by the Indians on January 23rd. He was never heard from again.

George Madison, born in Virginia, served in the American Revolution as a boy. He then moved to Kentucky. Serving during the Indian wars of the 1790's, he was wounded several times and eventually obtained the rank of Major in the 1st Rifle Regiment. After the losses on the 22nd of January, Major Madison was the highest-ranking officer left on the field. It was he who negotiated the final terms of surrender to the British. His captivity in Quebec ruined his health. In 1816 he was elected Governor of Kentucky, but died of tuberculosis shortly after taking his oath of office.

[26] Jean-Baptiste Jerome was the father-in-law of Hubert LaCroix. His farm was located on the west side of Jean-Baptiste Couture's farm. Jerome's house was the site of the first local district court held in 1805. His house was used as a hospital during the battles of Frenchtown and was burned to the ground on the 23rd

[27] John Allen was born in Virginia and arrived in Kentucky when he was 8 years old. As an adult, Allen moved to Virginia and practiced law until 1795. He moved back to Kentucky and was a member of the

Kentucky legislature from 1800 until 1810. He ran for Governor of Kentucky in 1808, but lost. At the beginning of the war of 1812, Allen raised one of the first regiments in the state. On June 5, 1812, he became Lt. Colonel of the 1st Rifle Regiment.

At Frenchtown, Allen was killed leading reinforcements to strengthen the retreating right wing. An Indian chief saw Allen during the retreat and decided to save the soldier because of his bravery. The Indians surrounded Allen, and one native advanced upon him. Allen drew his sword and killed him with one blow. A second Indian, ignoring the chief's orders, shot him dead.

[28] At one time Peter Navarre, son of Utreau Navarre, resided with his parents at the River Raisin, but by the War of 1812, they were all living at Presque Isle near the Ottawa village at the mouth of the Maumee. Peter's knowledge of the area made him an excellent scout, and he served in this capacity throughout the war. Today, Peter Navarre is generally regarded as the founder of Toledo, Ohio.

[29] It is not documented where Etienne was at this point in time. He may have stayed in Frenchtown, or he may not. We placed him here so we could show you both battles through his eyes. The accounts we have for the following chapter would lead us to believe that he was not at Sandy Creek after the first battle.

Besides being angry with the British and Indians for confiscating or looting property, there may have been another motivation for the young men of the River Raisin to violate their parole and take up arms against the British. When Frenchtown was surrendered in 1812, one group of local cavalrymen led by Cornet Isaac Lee refused to participate. They fled south to continue the fight from American held territory. The majority were from Anglo-American families, men like James Knaggs, who had a price on his head, and James Bentley, who had deserted from the British army many years before the war. Exaggerated stories of their exploits during the American raid on the Indian villages at Mississinewa may have led some of those still at the River Raisin to want to follow their example.

[30] Gandon's property was at Sandy Creek along the road leading to Detroit. The proximity of his farm made his residence a familiar stopping point for Indians and others going to and from Detroit. Francois Gandon and his family were not at home during the battles and therefore were safe from Indian attacks. The family eventually

returned from Detroit and found the house, barn and fruit trees destroyed and their livestock stolen or killed. Gandon's wife refused to live on the farm ever again because of the skeletons they found in the ruins, and poor Gandon had to exchange his property for a less valuable one further up the creek.

[31] There are over half a dozen variations of this story in print. Some refer to the father, René LeBeau, as Achan Labo or Etienne Labo Sr., and another refers to him as Achan Leboo. One version, preserved by the Laboe descendants, even has young Etienne present in the house and chopping off one of the Indian's hands with an ax. This version also suggests that the killers were not strangers to Soleau and LeBeau.

It is not impossible that the killings on Sandy Creek were out of revenge and feelings of betrayal. Many of the habitants did fight alongside the Ketuckians against their Potawatomi neighbors on January 18th. Some of the Indians found this American loyalty hard to understand. For example, during that fight on the 18th, Jacques Navarre captured 2 Indians who had strayed off from their comrades. They allowed him to approach, thinking he was one of their own until he grabbed their weapons and told them they were his prisoners. His brother Peter and Benac, a local resident, were approaching as one of the warriors attempted to escape. Benac shot him dead.

Regardless of which version is used, the essential story of the children's flight to Frenchtown remains the same, however, and we have tried to present the scenario in its most likely form.

[32] Alexis Loranger came to the River Raisin from Detroit about 1800 and succeeded Etienne Dubois as official singer of the parish in 1802. He led the choir and, in the absence of the priest, made all public announcements, taught religion, and kept records. He did not marry until 1818, well after the war was over.

The Loranger family was prominent in both Detroit and Frenchtown. Joseph Loranger purchased the land for the Courthouse Square and laid out the first village plat after the County of Monroe was formed in 1817.

[33] Jean-Baptiste Romain dit Sans Crainte II, was born in Montreal in 1754. His father, a soldier at Fort Michilimackinac, was present at the 1763 massacre and later moved to Vincennes. His wife Margaret Soleau was Jean-Baptiste Soleau's aunt. During the American Revolution, according to local legend, Sanscrainte was captured with a

party of British-allied Indians at Vincennes by George Rogers Clark. Dressed and painted like the Indians, he would have been executed as a renegade had not his father, who was with the American forces, not recognized him and reluctantly interceded on his behalf. (Most likely this was a story Sanscrainte told as an eyewitness, but not about himself.)

Nonetheless, Sanscrainte did work with the British Indian Department during both the Revolutionary War and the War of 1812. He was also an interpreter for the Americans in the 1790's and employed by them as a scout or spy during the first 2 months of the War of 1812. By the time of the Battle of the River Raisin, he was back on the British side. Both his sons, one of whom was also named Jean-Baptiste, fought on the American side. It is therefore possible that the Jean-Baptiste who led the patrol to recover the bodies of Soleau and LeBeau was one of his sons, rather than himself, although it seems unlikely that the younger Sanscrainte would have taken charge of the patrol as claimed.

The elder Sanscrainte died in 1828, alone, in his 70's, while out hunting for wild horses along the Coldwater River. It is supposed he was drinking, got groggy, fell off his horse, and died of exposure. In death, as in life, mystery surrounds this shadowy runner of the woods. When his body was found, wolves had eaten away the face, and he was only identified by his clothing.

[34] Medard Labadie mentioned his participation in the patrol to recover the bodies of Soleau and LeBeau in an affidavit written after the war. He often went out scouting with James Knaggs, had a British price on his head, and was one of those who claimed to recognize the body of Tecumseh after the Battle of the Thames.

The other members of the patrol, Jean-Baptiste Sanscrainte, Alexis Sanscrainte, Joseph Menard, Joseph LaTour, and the Nadeau brothers, were all mentioned in a curiously confusing document written by a descendant, Charles F. Soncrant.

Alexis was a son of Jean-Baptiste Sancrainte II and had been a fellow volunteer with Etienne LeBeau in LaCroix's Company of River Raisin militiamen. Joseph Menard dit Montour may have been from one of the Sandy Creek families and had been captain of the company formed from residents downriver on the River Raisin.

Antoine, Baptiste, and Joseph Nadeau were the sons of Martin Nadeau and are all listed on the roster of Captain Jean-Baptiste Couture's militia company which had been formed from those families living north of the River Raisin. No Joseph LaTour was listed, but there was a J. B. LaTour on the roster. The younger Jean-Baptiste Sanscrainte was also in this company.

Their scout, Joseph Navarre, is another mystery. There are plenty of references to a Jacques or James Navarre, but none to any Joseph of the right age and in the right location. If we do assume Soncrant was referring to a Jacques Navarre, there were 3 of them in the area to choose from. The authors prefer the brother of Peter Navarre who is known to have been present during the battles on both the 18th and 22nd, serving as a scout for the Kentuckians.

[35] Marie Suzor Navarre was born at Assumption, in Sandwich, Upper Canada, in 1772, the daughter of Louis Suzor and Marie Josephine LeBeau (René LeBeau's sister.) In 1790, she married Francois Navarre in Detroit. Their 14th child was born in 1815. Francois died of cholera in 1826. Marie died of the same disease in 1834, although some accounts have her dying the same year as her husband, whose death date & burial site are also in dispute.

As for Colonel Francois Navarre, he remained actively working for the American cause throughout the war and held a highly respected position in postwar society, bridging the gap between the French and English speaking populations of Monroe County. He is still fondly remembered as the founder of Monroe.

[36] Brigadier General James Winchester was born in Maryland in 1752 and served in the Revolutionary War. Moving to Tennessee in 1785, he saw further service against the Indians, rising in rank from captain to brigadier general. He also was elected to the State Senate.

During the War of 1812, he commanded the Left Wing of the Army of the Northwest, but was defeated and captured at the Battle of the River Raisin. Upon his release, he was placed in command of the Mobile District. He resigned his commission at the end of the war and spent the next several years trying to defend himself against charges of military incompetence.

In 1819, Winchester was appointed commissioner to run the Tennessee-Mississippi boundary line. He then retired to his plantation of Cragfont, where he was involved in public affairs and real estate, helping lay out the City of Memphis. In a curious parallel with the life of his former River Raisin host, Francois Navarre, he, too, raised 14 children and died in 1826.

[37] Dr. John Todd was born in Kentucky in 1787. He was the uncle of Mary Todd, who would later marry Abraham Lincoln. Todd was a surgeon with the 5th Kentucky when captured at the River Raisin. After the war, he returned to Kentucky, practicing medicine in Lexington and Bardstown. In 1817, he moved to Illinois, dying in Springfield in 1865.

[38] Captain Nathaniel Gray Smith Hart was born in Maryland in 1784. His father, a colonel and Revolutionary War veteran, moved the family to Lexington, Kentucky in 1794. Nathaniel became a lawyer and businessman, and, in 1812, commanded the Lexington Light Infantry.

Since his sister Lucretia was married to Senator Henry Clay, there was quite an investigation into his death at the River Raisin. Hart had been wounded during the fight on January 22 and had been left behind with the other wounded Kentuckians when the British retreated northward after the battle. When the Indians returned on the 23rd, Hart offered a Potawatomi named Osamed $100 to take him safely to Detroit. On the way, his captor got into an argument with some Wyandots. Despite Osamed's objections, Hart was shot, tomahawked and scalped, and his plundered body was left lying in the road. Henri Chauvin, whose own son lay dead in the road a mile beyond, covered Hart's body with bark. That night, Chauvin, Couture, and several others defied Indian threats and buried the body in a hollow made by the roots of a fallen tree. Years later, a delegation visited the spot and removed Hart's jawbone, which they returned to Kentucky.

[39] There was one drummer listed as killed during the battle. He was Jesse Cock in Kerley's Company of the 1st Rifle Regiment. We don't know his age, or anything else about him, but he may someday figure as a main character in another work on the battle.

[40] Medard Couture stayed with his father, Capt. Jean-Baptiste Couture, to defend their home while the rest of the family escaped to the house of Francois Navarre before the British & Indian assault on January 22. Both apparently joined the reinforcements sent out from the picketted gardens of Frenchtown to bolster the retreating right wing of the American army. Jean-Baptiste was probably killed somewhere in the vicinity of the Robert house across the river, and Medard brought his father's body back to their yard after the surrender of the Kentuckians, hoping to conceal it from the Indians. He then stayed to help the

American doctors care for the wounded Kentuckians who had been left behind in Frenchtown when the British retreated northward.

On January 23, some 200 Indians returned to Frenchtown and began seizing the wounded Americans, killing many of them, and setting fire to the buildings, including the Couture house. Stripped and tied by a band of Chippewa who left him standing in the snow near the blazing ruins of the Jerome house, Medard was only saved by the intervention of his friend, Waugon, an elderly Ottawa chief. Waugon told his men to find him some clothes, saying, "Take care of him…He is my son. His father lies dead in the yard, and I am now his father…"

[41] Alexis Platte Navarre was about 15 years old when he helped transport the Navarre family to Detroit. This incident took place either on the night of the 22nd or the 23rd. We used it in our story as the vehicle for getting the LeBeau children out of Frenchtown, although, in truth, we don't really know how they actually got to Detroit.

In 1814, Platte Navarre married Therese Beauregard, another refugee from the River Raisin. The young couple eventually returned to St-Antoine's Parish and had 11 children before he died in 1873.

[42] Rachel Sly Knaggs came to the Maumee Valley with her husband, George, as early as the 1760's, where all 8 of her children were born. George Knaggs was an Indian trader and British sympathizer, but his Maumee trading post was burned by Anthony Wayne's American troops in 1794, and the family relocated to Detroit and the River Raisin.

Rachel became a widow in 1797, although it is unclear if George actually died or simply ran off to sea. In any case, by the War of 1812, the Knaggs family had become solidly anti-British.

After the war, Rachel returned to the River Raisin, but eventually left her property there to her children. She died in Green Bay during one of her periodic visits to a store she had opened there which dealt in furs and bear oil.

[43] Elizabeth Anderson, daughter of Rachel Knaggs, was born in 1772. Her most famous exploit during the War of 1812 came after her husband, Col. John Anderson, had to flee the wrath of the Indians, leaving her behind to care for their 3 children and the trading post.

When the Indians came to the trading post, they found her sitting on a chest with her 3-year-old son, Alexander, on her lap. Unknown to the Indians, the chest contained over $800 in gold and silver. At one point, one of the Indians told her to stand up and threatened her with his tomahawk. She dared him to strike a lone woman, and the Indian, respecting her bravery, backed down.

There are probably a dozen versions of this story, but the earliest written record in the Monroe Museum Archives appeared in her obituary in the <u>Monroe Commercial</u> newspaper, February 9, 1854. Most historians place the incident in January, during the 1813 battles. However, a strong case can be made for August of 1812 when there are several independent reports of her being harassed and plundered by the Indians. Furthermore, there is some reason to believe she was already living in Detroit by January of 1813.

[44] The local habitants had been under pressure to join the Indian cause since the previous year when Wyandot chiefs Roundhead and Walk-in-the-Water had sent the following message: "Friends, listen! You have always told us you would give us any assistance in your power. We...call upon you all to rise up...bringing your arms along with you. Should you fail this time, we will not consider you in the future as friends, and the consequences may be very unpleasant..."

Although a minority, there were some who did answer the Indians' call in those days before the battle. The most prominent was Jacko Lasselle, a fur trader who had married Marie Bluejacket, a Shawnee. When Winchester's force arrived at the Raisin, he disputed the reports of other habitants that the British were capable of mounting a serious counterattack. Secretly, however, he sent Young Bluejacket with a message to the British at Fort Malden, detailing the situation of the Kentuckians. The letter was drafted by his daughter Nanette, who later married Thomas Caldwell, one of the Canadian officers who fought on the British side at the Battle of the River Raisin.

On several occasions, the British authorities tried to convince their Indian allies to destroy the settlement completely, but the Potawatomies always objected, arguing it was they, the Potawatomies, who had given the habitants their lands, for which they had been compensated, and they would not allow them to be forced to leave.

Of course, over half the population fled Frenchtown after the battle of January 22. The main refugee centers for the River Raisin families were at Detroit, in British held territory, or at Sandusky, which was under American control. The evening before the battle, for example, Louis LaFountain, Laurent Durocher, Joseph Loranger, and John Beaugrand were playing cards at Loranger's store house when an Indian arrived to warn them of the approach of Procter's army. LaFountain went to get his family and took them to Detroit, while

Durocher and Beaugrand headed for Sandusky, where their wives had previously been sent for safety. The next month, Durocher and Loranger joined the American army at Fort Meigs, serving in Antoine Couture's loosely organized company of scouts. Apparently, conditions at Sandusky were not good for the French, so many of them moved a second time, up into British territory.

[45] The muskrat has played a starring role in the history of Monroe County since prehistoric times when native peoples ate them and used their fur. Early French trappers and traders who ventured into the River Raisin Country adopted the Indian custom, along with many other native ways, to the extent that their descendants became known as the Muskrat French. When other food supplies gave out during the War of 1812, it was the muskrat who kept our community from starvation. In many Monroe families, the tradition of eating muskrat on special occasions has been kept up, and local clubs and churches are still serving seasonal muskrat dinners from January through early March.

M'Sieur le Musquash, also known as the marsh rabbit or the Grand Seigneur of the marshes, has been the subject of a number of local poems and legends. One tale explained how the muskrat could be eaten as a fish on Catholic fasting days, since it spent so much time in the water. Many locals believed the Pope himself had granted permission to do this, although no record of it has been found in the Papal archives.

The most traditional way to consume the little beast is by roasting it in corn, but people often developed their own favorite recipes. German and Polish immigrants even cooked it with sauerkraut. As one early chef put it, "Fry it wid' honions, you shan't tole it from duck."

[46] The War of 1812 officially ended when the Treaty of Ghent was signed on Christmas Eve, 1814. Unfortunately, news traveled so slowly that the fighting continued into the following year. In fact, one of the most famous battles of the war, Andrew Jackson's victory at the Battle of New Orleans took place on January 8, 1815. The treaty did not put an immediate end to the bad feelings between Canadian loyalists and American republicans, but it did require the return by both sides of captured territory and laid the foundations for a lasting peace.

[47] In October of 1813, when American troops were consolidating their control of the lower Great Lakes, Lt. Col. Lewis Cass replaced the discredited William Hull as governor of Michigan Territory.

[48] James Monroe served President Madison as both Secretary of State and Secretary of War during the War of 1812. In 1816, Monroe became the 5th President of the United States. As President, he launched the Era of Good Feeling, but also established the Monroe Doctrine to keep European countries from interfering in the affairs of the Western Hemisphere.

He was also the first President to visit Michigan, at which time the River Raisin country was being formed into a new county. Governor Cass named this county Monroe, in honor of the President's visit. It seems, however, that President Monroe stayed in Detroit, never bothering to visit the county named for him.

[49] The linguistic abilities of our early settlers are well documented. We know the locals were still competent in native languages as late as 1846, when Charles Lanman recorded a conversation between Antoine Campeau and a French hunter named Benac. The two made use of no less than three languages, which Lanman described as "bad French, broken English, and genuine Potawattomee."

As for the local French dialect, an 1897 study by the University of Michigan found it to be quite good, albeit a bit old-fashioned and suffering from the effects of over a century of isolation from the parent tongue. It was spoken in some of our outlying farming communities until well into the 20th century.

[50] These bones led archaeologists to the discovery of the entire cemetery of St. Antoine's Church. Despite old stories that all the bodies had been removed to a new cemetery, a careful scraping of the top layer of earth in the vicinity revealed 35 graves. Another 45 graves were found by a dog trained to locate human remains. Negotiations followed between the city, the developer, the church, and interested citizens to decide the future of this forgotten graveyard.

A Native Warrior, Winter, 1813
by Joe Lee